VICTORIAN ARCHITECTURAL DETAILS

Designs for Over 700 Stairs, Mantels, Doors, Windows, Cornices, Porches, and other Decorative Elements

A. J. BICKNELL & COMPANY

DOVER PUBLICATIONS, INC.
Mineola, New York

NOTE

For the present edition, the original plates have been reduced to better fit the trim size of this book.

Bibliographical Note

This Dover edition, first published in 2005, is an unabridged republication, with a slight reduction, of the work originally published by A. J. Bicknell & Co., New York, in 1873 under the title *Detail, Cottage and Constructive Architecture: Containing 75 Large Lithographic Plates.*

Library of Congress Cataloging-in-Publication Data

Detail, cottage and constructive architecture.
    Victorian architectural details : designs for over 700 stairs, mantels, doors, windows, cornices, porches, and other decorative elements / A.J. Bicknell & Company.
        p. cm.
    Originally published: Detail, cottage and constructive architecture : containing 75 large lithographic plates. New York : A.J. Bicknell & Co., 1873.
    ISBN-13: 978-0-486-44015-6 (pbk.)
    ISBN-10: 0-486-44015-X (pbk.)
    1. Architecture, Victorian—United States—Designs and plans. 2. Architecture, Domestic—United States—Designs and plans. 3. Architecture—Details. I. Bicknell, A. J. (Amos Jackson). Detail, cottage and constructive architecture. II. William T. Comstock Company. III. Title.

NA7207.D47 2004
729'.097309034—dc22

                                                                    2004059327

Manufactured in the United States by LSC Communications
44015X06   2017
www.doverpublications.com

Detail, Cottage and Constructive Architecture.

LIST OF PLATES.

FRONTISPIECE.—Block of Four Stores; Style, English Gothic.

Plates 1, 2, 3 and 4.—Twenty-eight Designs and Illustrations for Cornices and Belt Courses.

Plate 5.—Eighteen Designs and Illustrations for Cornices and Brackets.

Plate 6.—Twelve Designs for Brackets.

Plate 7.—Twelve Designs and Illustrations for Brick Cornices and Chimney Tops.

Plate 8.—Stone Cottage, with Brick Dressings.

Plate 9.—Nineteen Designs for Windows.

Plate 10.—Twenty Designs for Windows.

Plate 11.—Fourteen Designs and Illustrations for Window Caps.

Plate 12.—Ten Designs and Illustrations for Dormer Windows.

Plate 13.—Twenty-seven Designs, Details and Sections of Bay and Dormer Windows.

Plate 14.—Oriel Bay and Dormer Windows.

Plate 15.—Design for Cottage; Style, Domestic Gothic.

Plate 16.—Detail of Design, Plate 15.

Plate 17.—Four Designs for Front Doors.

Plate 18.—Six Designs for Interior Finish for Doors and Windows.

Plate 19.—Design for Interior Finish for Doors, Windows and Wainscoting.

Plate 20.—Twenty Designs and Details for Door and Window Finish.

Plate 21.—Villa, two Cottages, Summer House, Well House and Fencing.

Plate 22.—Plans and Details of Italian Villa, shown on Plate 21.

Plate 23.—Eleven Designs and Illustrations for Piazzas.

Plate 24.—Four Designs for Piazzas.

Plate 25.—Two Designs and Details for Piazzas.

Plate 26.—Design for a Porch, with Balcony, showing Front and Vestibule Doors.

Plate 27.—Designs and Detail of Veranda and Porch.

Plate 28.—Design of Suburban Residence.

Plate 29.—Detail of Design, shown on Plate 28.

Plate 30.—Design for Observatory and Towers.

Plate 31.—Five Designs for Balconies, Canopies and Porches.

Plate 32.—Two Designs for Sawed Ornaments.

Plate 33.—Four Designs for Gable Ornaments.

Plate 34.—Ten Designs for Sawed Ornaments.

Plate 35.—Fifty-three Designs and Illustrations for Scrolls and Brackets.

Plate 36.—Perspective View, Front and Side Elevations and Plans of Suburban Residence.

Plate 37.—Two Designs for Gables, in the Modern Swiss Style.

Plate 38.—Four Designs for Fences.

Plate 39.—Two Designs for Stairs.

Plate 40.—Fifteen Designs for Newels, Hand Rails and Balusters.

Plate 41.—Design for Suburban Cottage.

Plate 42.—Details of Design, Plate 41.

Plate 43.—Twenty-six Designs for Architraves and Base, and Seven Designs for Plaster Cornices.

Plate 44.—Six Designs for Plaster Cornices and Ceilings.

Plate 45.—Designs for Mantels and Mantel with Mirror.

Plate 46.—Designs for One-Story French Cottage, with Tower.

Plate 47.—Details of Design, Plate 46.

Plate 48.—Designs for a Swiss Summer House, etc.

Plate 49.—Design for Swiss Porch, Balconies, etc.

Plate 50.—Design and Section for a Two-Story Suburban Residence.

Plate 51.—Details of Design, Plate 50.

Plate 52.—Designs for Street Fronts for Dwellings.

Plate 53.—Design for French Flat.

Plate 54.—Two-Story French Roof and Basement, arranged for two families.

Plate 55.—Designs for One-Story Store Fronts.

Plate 56.—Designs for Store Fronts.

Plate 57.—Designs for Store Fronts.

Plate 58.—Fittings for Stores.

Plate 59.—Fittings for Stores.

Plate 60.—Designs for Banking Houses and Store Counters.

Plate 61.—Designs for Bank Counters and Office Screens.

Plates 62 and 63.—Design for Gothic Cottage, with Tower.

Plate 64.—Framing of Design, Plate 62 and 63.

Plate 65.—Design for Two-Story Cottage.

Plate 66.—Balloon Frame for Small Cottage.

Plate 67.—Frame for Gothic Residence.

Plate 68.—Frame for Small Double House, with Mansard Roof.

Plate 69.—Frame for a Small Side Hill Barn.

Plate 70.—Frame for a Large Barn.

Plate 71.—Frame for Exhibition Buildings.

Plate 72.—Framing for Roofs.

Plate 73.—Framing for Bridges.

Plate 74.—Nine Elevations for Cottages and Villas.

Plate 75.—Six Elevations of Summer Houses and Sea Side Cottages.

DESIGNS FOR CORNICES.

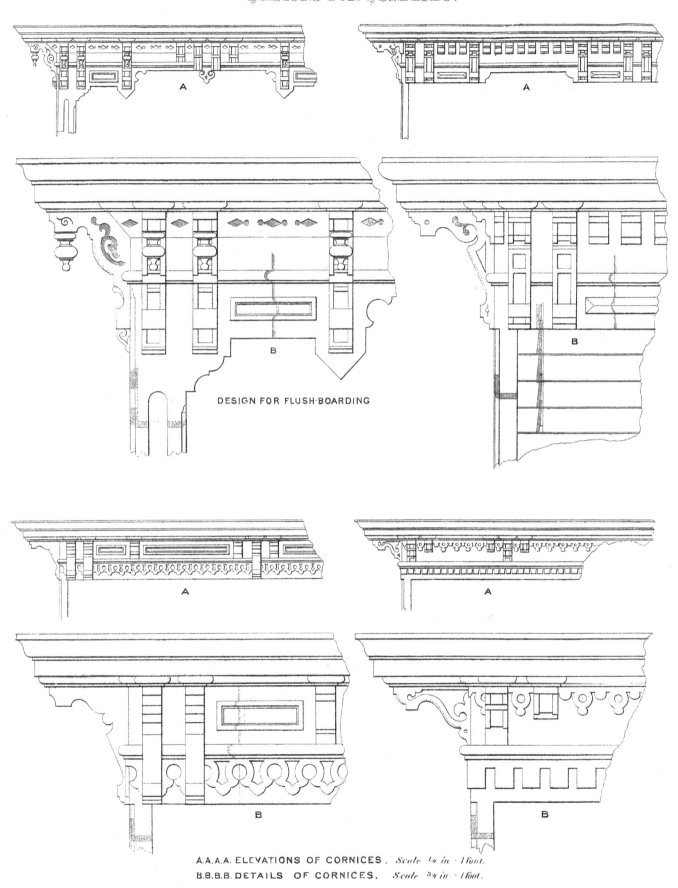

DESIGN FOR FLUSH-BOARDING

A.A.A.A. ELEVATIONS OF CORNICES. *Scale ¼ in = 1 foot.*
B.B.B.B. DETAILS OF CORNICES. *Scale ¾ in = 1 foot.*

PLATE 1

Scale: ¾ in = 1 foot.

PLATE 2

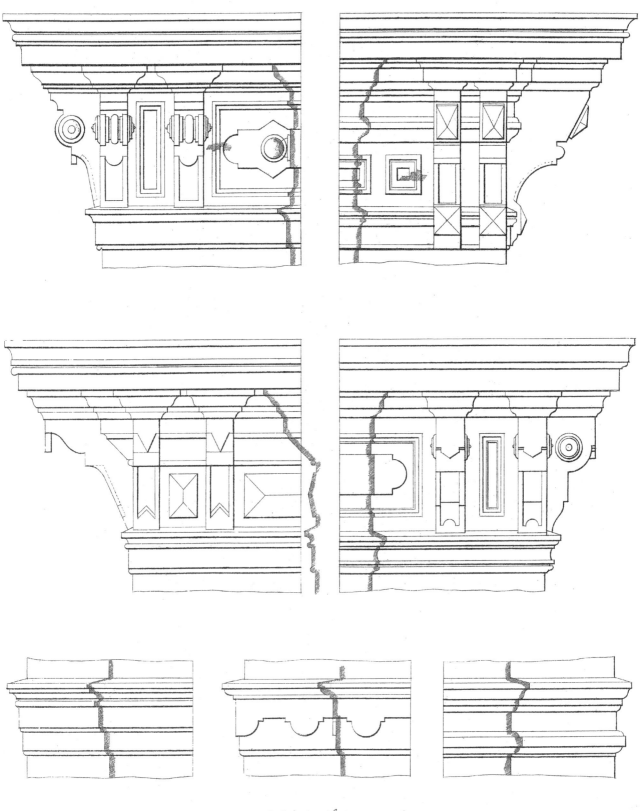

Scale ³⁄₄ in. = 1 foot.

Plate 3

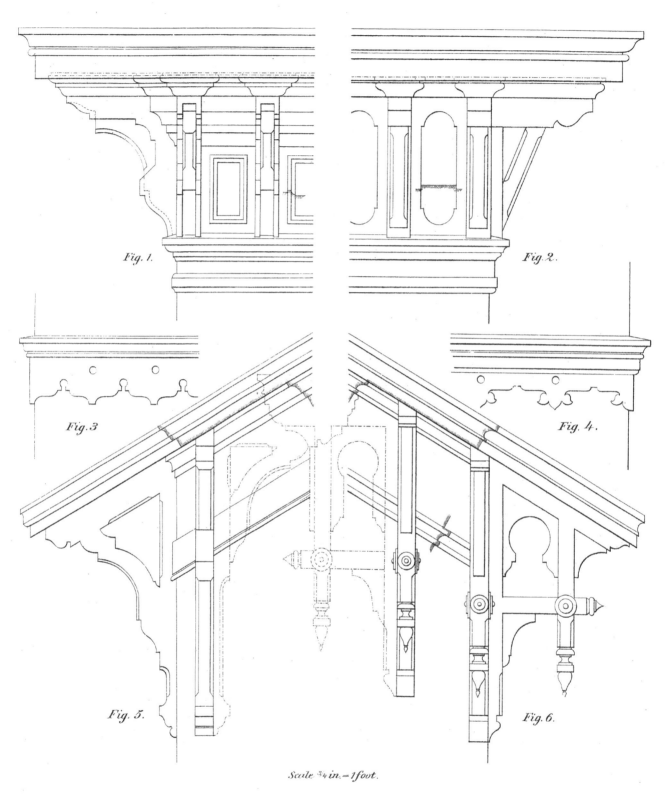

Fig. 1.

Fig. 2.

Fig. 3

Fig. 4.

Fig. 5.

Fig. 6.

Scale ¾ in. = 1 foot.

The dotted lines in Fig. 5 & Fig. 6 indicate the Side Elevation of Brackets on Gable.

PLATE 4

DESIGNS FOR CORNICES AND BRACKETS.

Fig. 6

Fig. 1.

Verandah Bracket ½ in. Scale

Fig. 7

Fig 2

Fig. 3.

Fig. 10.

Fig. 4.

Fig. 8.

Fig. 5.

Fig. 9.

Fig. 1. Scale ½ in. = 1 foot.
Fig. 2.3.4.5. Scale ¾ in. = 1 foot.
Fig. 6.7.8.9.10. Brackets, Scale ¾ in. = 1 ft.

PLATE 5

Plate 6

Designs for Brick Cornices and Chimney Tops.

Section on E F

Parts marked W below to be formed of White Bricks.

Section on C D

Sheet Lead

Section on A B

Scale ½ in - one foot.

Plate 7

= Stone Cottage with Brick Dressings =

— Front Elevation —   — Side Elevation —

— Perspective View —

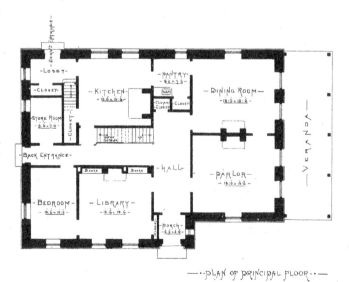

— Plan of Principal Floor —

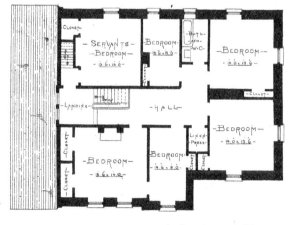

— Plan of Chamber Floor —

Scale of   Feet.   — Frederick C. Withers Architect —

Plate 8

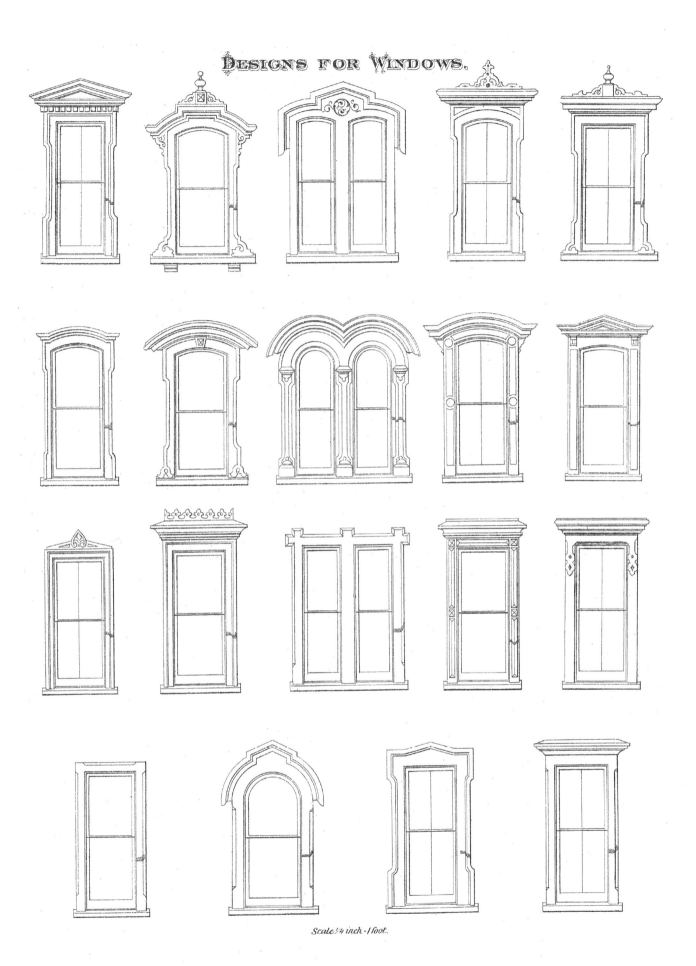

Scale ¼ inch = 1 foot.

PLATE 9

DESIGNS FOR WINDOWS.

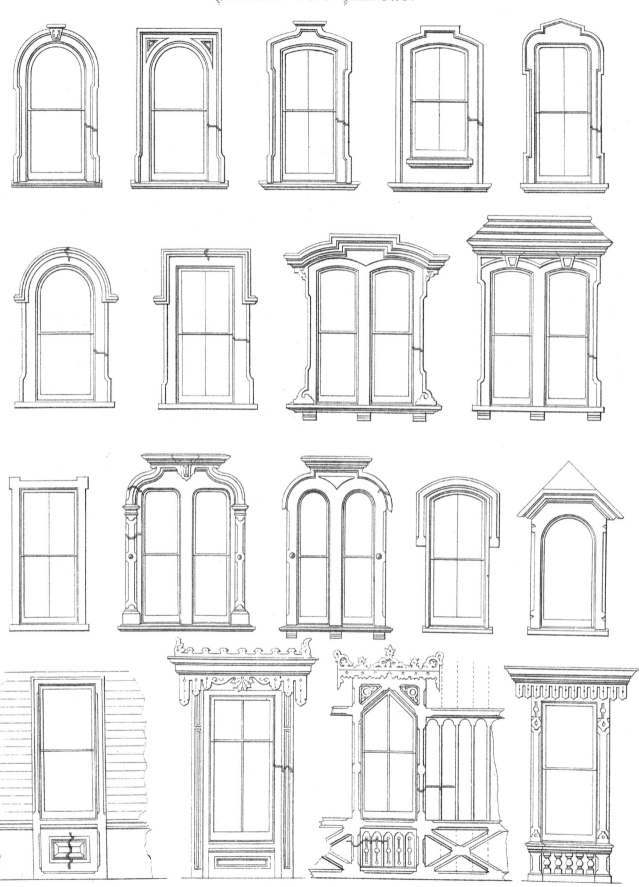

Scale ¼ in - one foot.

PLATE 10

SIDE ELEVATIONS.

FRONT ELEVATIONS.

FRONT ELEVATIONS.

Scale 3/4 in. = 1 foot.

PLATE 11

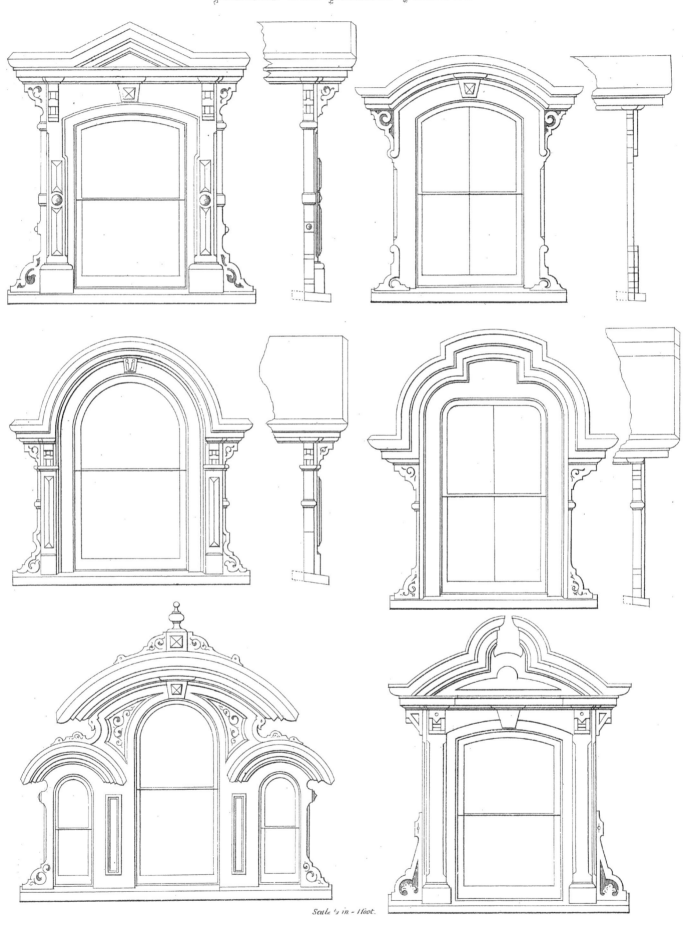

Scale ½ in - Foot.

Plate 12

DESIGNS FOR BAY AND DORMER WINDOWS

Fig. 1

Fig. 4

Fig. 6

Fig. 8

Fig. 13
Section

Fig. 11
Face
of Square Bay.

Fig. 12
End

Detail of Bay

Section of Bay

Bay

Bay

Fig. 2

Fig. 5

Fig. 7

Fig. 9

9' 9"

9' 9"

8' 6"

Fig. 3
Plan

Fig. 10
Plan

Fig. 14
Plan

Fig. 15

Fig. 16

Fig. 17

Fig. 20

Fig. 21

Fig. 22

Fig. 23

Fig. 15, 16, 17, 18 & 19 Details for Dormer Windows

Fig. 18

Fig. 19

Fig. 24

Fig. 25

Fig. 26

End View of Fig. 26
Fig. 27

Fig. 20, 21, 22, 23, 24, 25, 26. Dormer Windows.

Scale of Fig. 1 to 19. ½ in. = 1 foot.
"   "   " 20 to 27. ¼ "   "   "

PLATE 13

DESIGNS FOR ORIEL, BAY AND DORMER WINDOWS.

Fig.1

Fig.3

Fig. 4

Fig. 6

Fig.2

Fig.5

Fig.7

Fig.9

Fig.10

Fig.12

Fig.8

Fig.11

Fig.13

Fig.14

Fig.15

Fig.16

Fig.17

Fig.18

Fig.1 Oriel Window	Fig.4 Gothic Bay Window	Fig.7 High Bay Window	Fig.10 Low Bay Window	Fig.13 Small Dormer	Fig.16 Side of same
„ 2 Plan of do	„ 5 Plan of do	„ 8 Plan of do	„ 11 Plan of do	„ 14 Side of same	„ 17 Large Dormer
„ 3 Side of do	„ 6 Side of do	„ 9 Side of do	„ 12 Side of do	„ 15 French Dormer	„ 18 Side of same

Scale ⅛in = 1ft.

PLATE 14

SIDE ELEVATION.

FRONT ELEVATION.

DESIGN IN THE
DOMESTIC GOTHIC STYLE
BY
WILLIAM T. HALLETT
ARCHITECT.
Nº 111 Broadway, N.Y.

Scale ⅛ in. to 1 foot.

FIRST STORY PLAN.

W.C.
WOOD HOUSE
VERANDA
ENTRY
STORE
ENTRY
KITCHEN
14' x 14'
CHINA CLOSET
DINING ROOM
14' x 18'
PANTRY
SINK
RANGE
PASSAGE
PARLOUR
14' x 18'
HALL
18' x 14'
SITTING ROOM
14' x 18'
ARCADE
BALCONY
44'
39'

SECOND STORY PLAN.

W.C.
BED ROOM
7' x 8'
CHAMBER
14' x 14'
BATH ROOM
OWN CHAMBER
14' x 18'
BACK HALL
PRESS
PRESS
LINEN
PRESS
PRESS
GUEST CHAMBER
14' x 18'
HALL
18' x 14'
CHAMBER
14' x 16'
BALCONY

PLATE 15

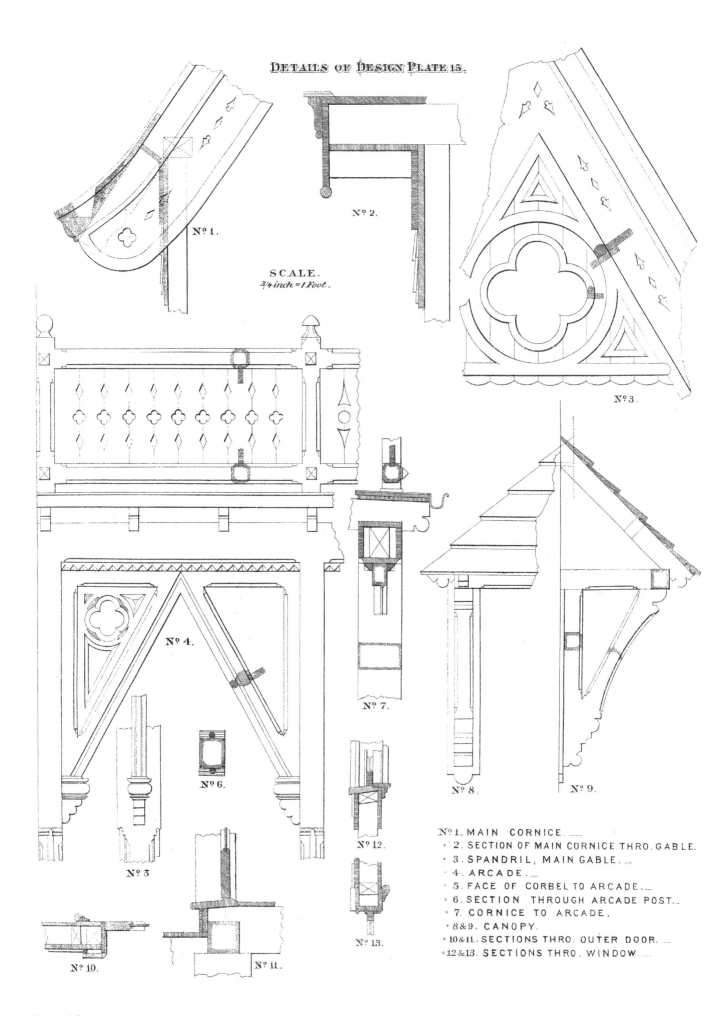

No 1.

No 2.

SCALE.
3/4 inch = 1 Foot.

No 3.

No 4.

No 5.

No 6.

No 7.

No 8.

No 9.

No 10.

No 11.

No 12.

No 13.

No 1. MAIN CORNICE.
" 2. SECTION OF MAIN CORNICE THRO. GABLE.
" 3. SPANDRIL, MAIN GABLE.
" 4. ARCADE.
" 5. FACE OF CORBEL TO ARCADE.
" 6. SECTION THROUGH ARCADE POST.
" 7. CORNICE TO ARCADE.
" 8 & 9. CANOPY.
" 10 & 11. SECTIONS THRO. OUTER DOOR.
" 12 & 13. SECTIONS THRO. WINDOW.

PLATE 16

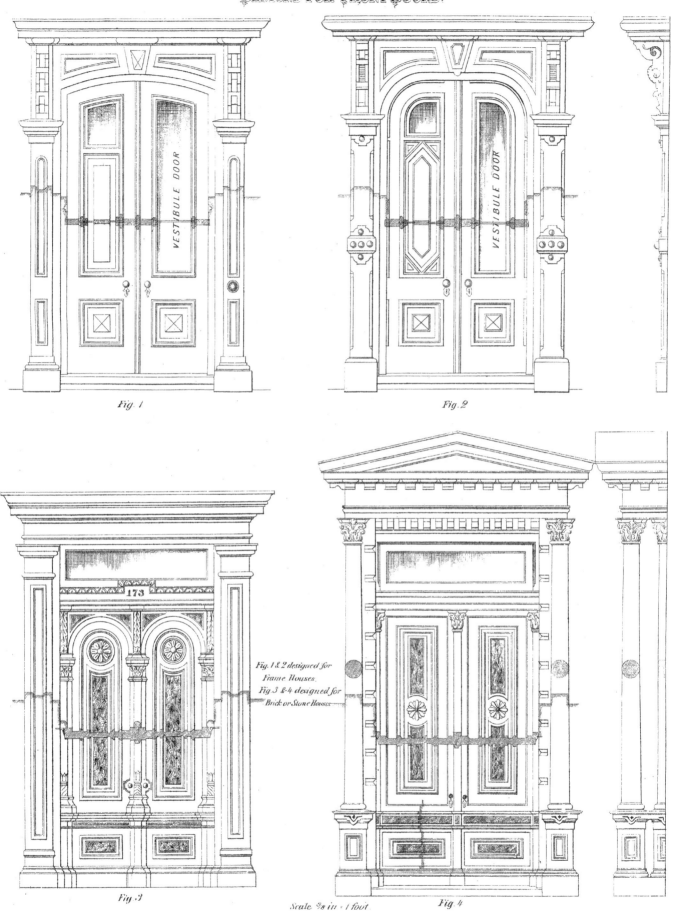

Fig. 1

Fig. 2

VESTIBULE DOOR

VESTIBULE DOOR

173

Fig. 1 & 2 designed for
Frame Houses.
Fig. 3 & 4 designed for
Brick or Stone Houses.

Fig. 3

Scale ⅜ in = 1 foot

Fig. 4

PLATE 17

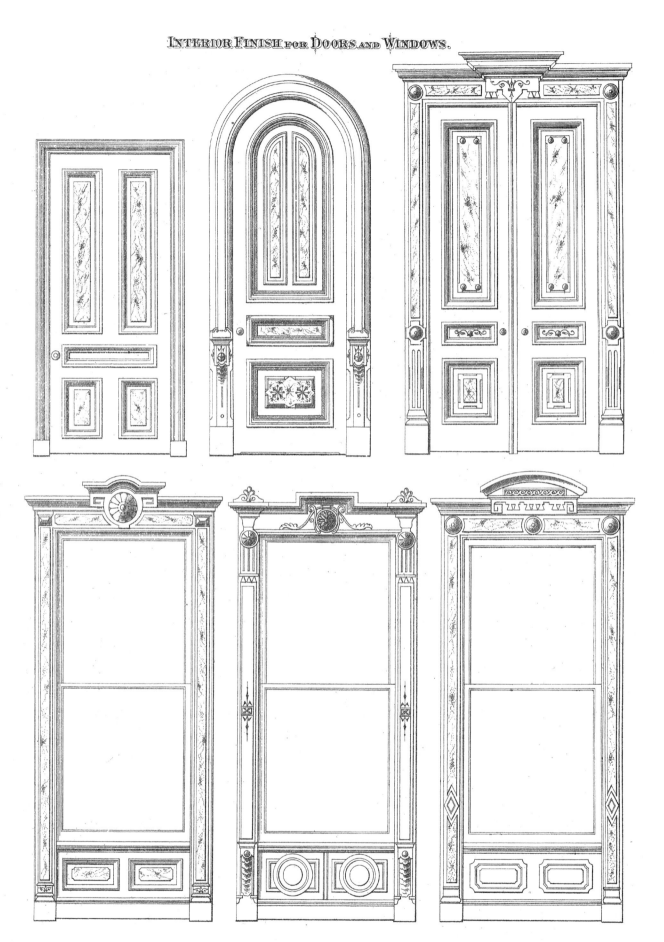

Scale: ½ inch = 1 foot.

PLATE 18

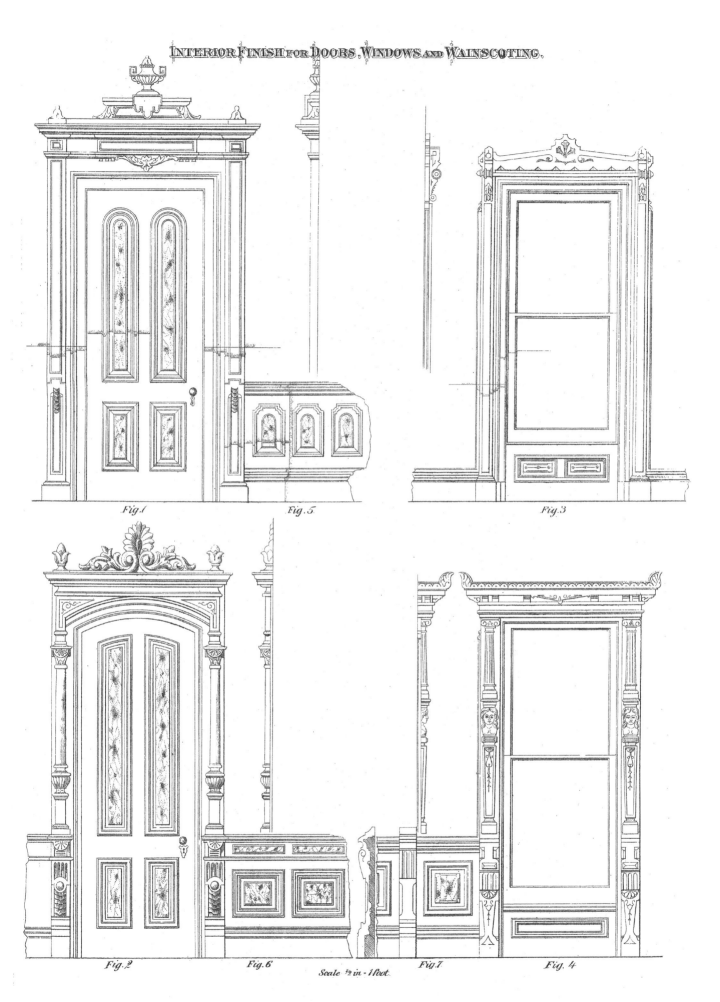

Fig. 1

Fig. 5

Fig. 3

Fig. 2

Fig. 6

Scale ½ in = 1 foot.

Fig. 7

Fig. 4

PLATE 19

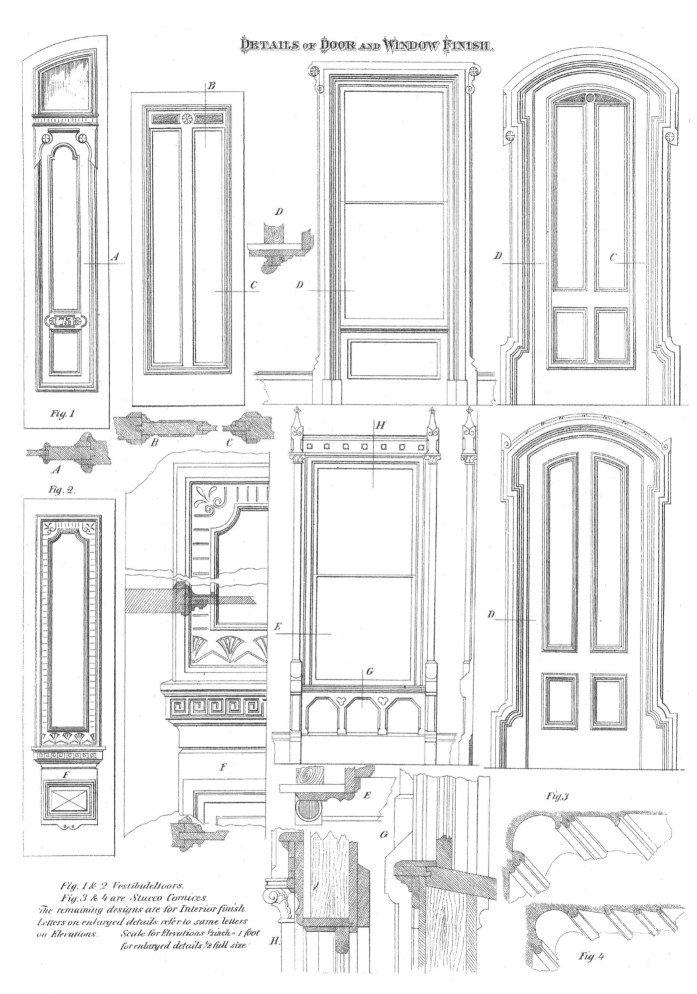

DETAILS OF DOOR AND WINDOW FINISH.

Fig. 1

Fig. 2

Fig. 3

Fig. 4

Fig. 1 & 2 Vestibule Doors.
Fig. 3 & 4 are Stucco Cornices.
The remaining designs are for Interior finish.
Letters on enlarged details refer to same letters
on Elevations.   Scale for Elevations ½ inch = 1 foot
            for enlarged details ⅛ full size.

PLATE 20

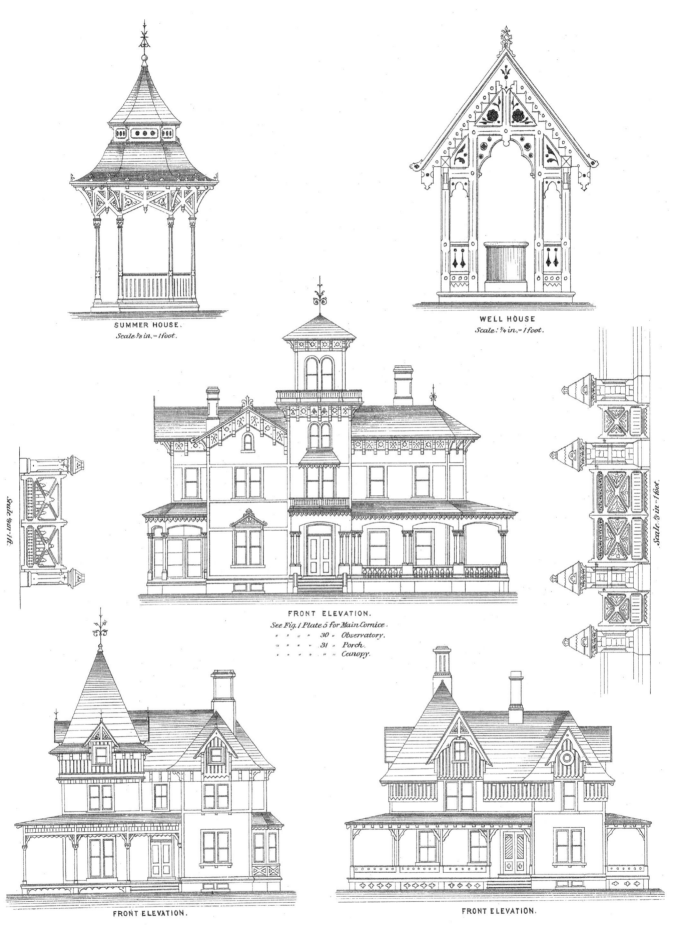

SUMMER HOUSE.

Scale ⅜ in. = 1 foot.

WELL HOUSE

Scale ¾ in. = 1 foot.

FRONT ELEVATION.

See Fig. 1 Plate 5 for Main Cornice.
" " " " 30 " Observatory.
" " " " 31 " Porch.
" " " " " Canopy.

FRONT ELEVATION.

FRONT ELEVATION.

Scale ⅛ in. = 1 ft.

H. HUDSON HOLLY, ARCHITECT, N.Y.

PLATE 21

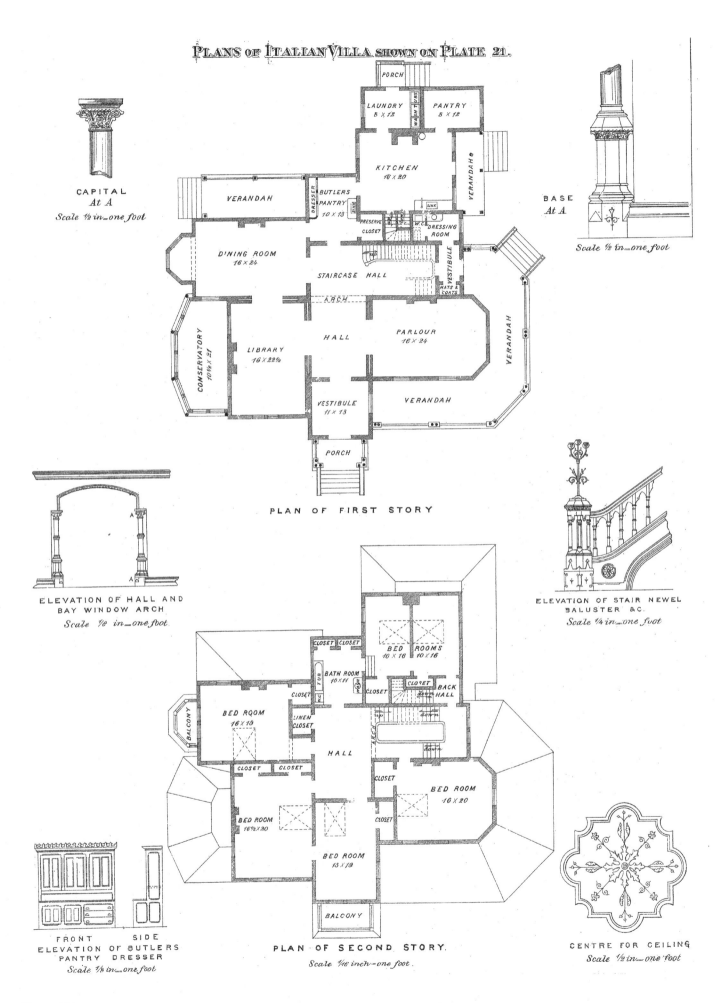

PLANS of ITALIAN VILLA shown on PLATE 21.

CAPITAL
At A
Scale ½ in—one foot

BASE
At A
Scale ½ in—one foot

PORCH

LAUNDRY
8 × 12

PANTRY
8 × 12

WASH TUBS

KITCHEN
16 × 20

VERANDAH

VERANDAH

BUTLERS
PANTRY
10 × 13

DRESSER

SINK

PRESERVE
CLOSET

W.C.

DRESSING
ROOM

VESTIBULE

DINING ROOM
16 × 24

STAIRCASE HALL

MATS &
COATS

ARCH

CONSERVATORY
10½ × 21

LIBRARY
16 × 22½

HALL

PARLOUR
16 × 24

VERANDAH

VESTIBULE
11 × 13

VERANDAH

PORCH

PLAN OF FIRST STORY

ELEVATION OF HALL AND
BAY WINDOW ARCH
Scale ⅛ in—one foot

ELEVATION OF STAIR NEWEL
BALUSTER &C.
Scale ¼ in—one foot

CLOSET CLOSET

BED ROOMS
10 × 16   10 × 16

BATH ROOM
10 × 11

BACK
HALL

CLOSET

CLOSET

TUB

W.C.

BALCONY

BED ROOM
16 × 19

LINEN
CLOSET

CLOSET

HALL

ARCH

DOWN

CLOSET

CLOSET

CLOSET

BED ROOM
16 × 20

BED ROOM
16½ × 20

CLOSET

BED ROOM
13 × 19

BALCONY

FRONT   SIDE
ELEVATION OF BUTLERS
PANTRY DRESSER
Scale ⅛ in—one foot

PLAN OF SECOND STORY.
Scale 1/16 inch—one foot

CENTRE FOR CEILING
Scale ½ in—one foot

PLATE 22

Scale ½ inch one foot.

PLATE 23

Scale: ½ inch one foot.

Plate 24

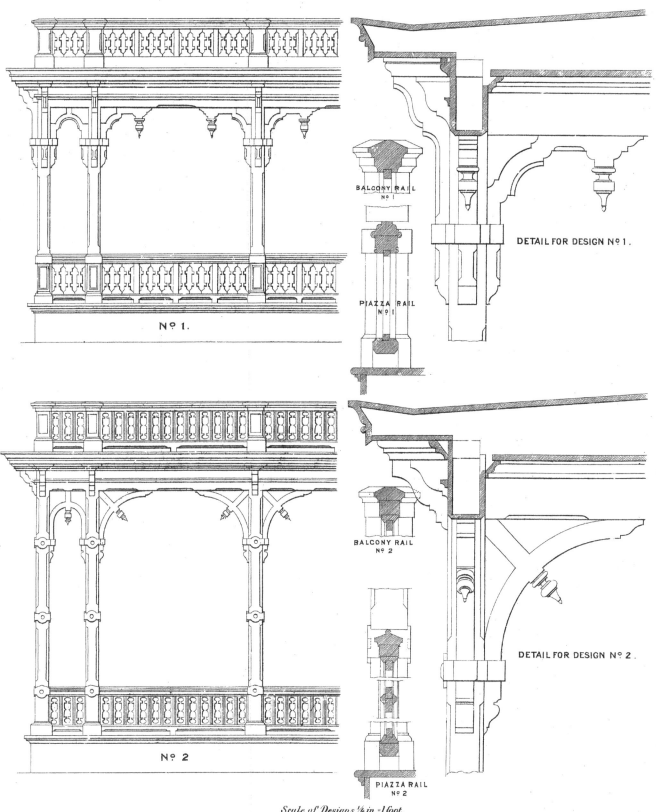

BALCONY RAIL
Nᵒ 1

PIAZZA RAIL
Nᵒ 1

DETAIL FOR DESIGN Nᵒ 1.

Nᵒ 1.

BALCONY RAIL
Nᵒ 2

PIAZZA RAIL
Nᵒ 2

DETAIL FOR DESIGN Nᵒ 2.

Nᵒ 2

Scale of Designs ¼ in = 1 foot.
Scale of Details ¾ in = 1 foot.

PLATE 25

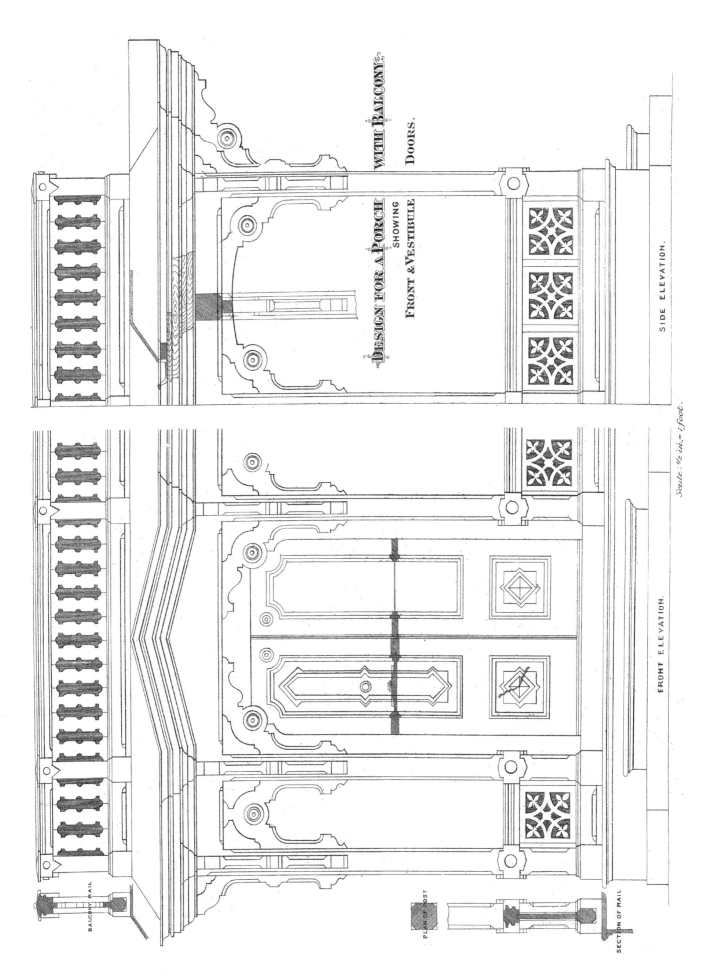

DESIGN FOR A PORCH
SHOWING
FRONT & VESTIBULE
WITH BALCONY,
DOORS.

SIDE ELEVATION.

Scale: ½ in. = 1 foot.

FRONT ELEVATION.

BALCONY RAIL

PLAN OF POST

SECTION OF RAIL

PLATE 26

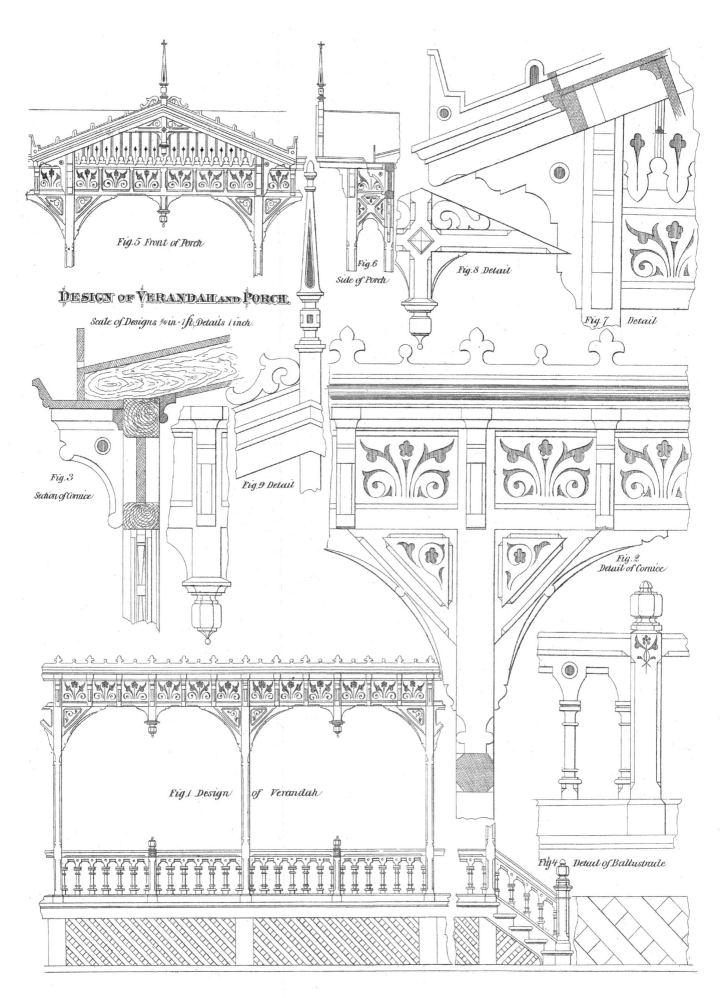

Fig.5 Front of Porch

Fig.6 Side of Porch

Fig.8 Detail

Fig.7 Detail

DESIGN OF VERANDAH AND PORCH.

Scale of Designs 1/4 in=1ft, Details 1 inch.

Fig.3 Section of Cornice

Fig.9 Detail

Fig.2 Detail of Cornice

Fig.1 Design of Verandah

Fig.4 Detail of Ballustrade

PLATE 27

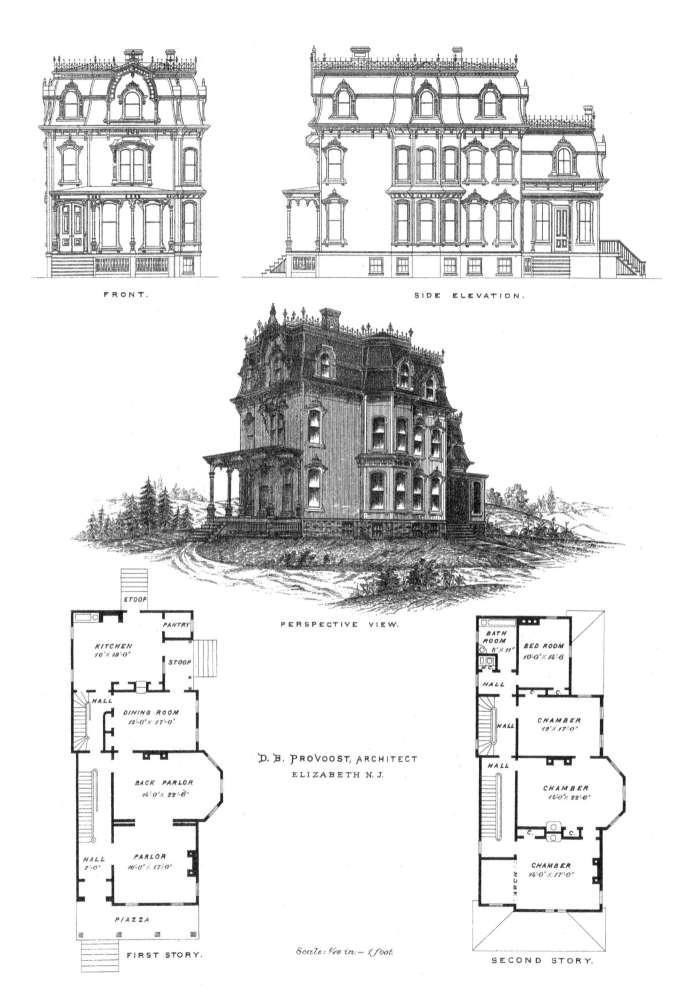

FRONT.

SIDE ELEVATION.

PERSPECTIVE VIEW.

STOOP

KITCHEN
16' X 19'-0"

PANTRY

STOOP

HALL

DINING ROOM
12'-0" X 17'-0"

BACK PARLOR
14'-0" X 22'-6"

HALL
7'-0"

PARLOR
16'-0" X 17'-0"

PIAZZA

FIRST STORY.

D. B. PROVOOST, ARCHITECT
ELIZABETH N. J.

Scale: 1/10 in. = 1 foot.

BATH
ROOM
8' X 11"
W.C.

BED ROOM
10'-0" X 14'-6

HALL

HALL

CHAMBER
12' X 17'-0"

HALL

CHAMBER
14'-0" X 22'-6"

ARCH

CHAMBER
14'-0" X 17'-0"

SECOND STORY.

PLATE 28

LINE OF ROOF

RAFTERS

RAFTER
2½"× 7"

1¾" SPRUCE PLANK

2"× 4"

PLASTER

JOIST

SHEATING

Scale of Designs: ½ in. = 1 foot.
Scale of Details: 1 in. = 1 foot.

A&B. FRENCH ROOF and CONSTRUCTION. ___
C&D. DORMER WINDOWS. ___
E&F. SIDE VIEW of DORMERS. ___
G.G. DECK CORNICE ___
H.H. BRACKETTS. ___
I.I. RETURN on DORMERS. ___
J.J. FOOT SCROLL. ___

K. SECTION of DORMER. ___
L.L. DORMER ORNAMENT. ___
m.m. HIP CASINGS. ___
n.n. ANGLE FINISH. ___
O.O. CORNICE, ___
P. BELT COURSE, ___
Q. TRUSS on DORMER. ___

PLATE 29

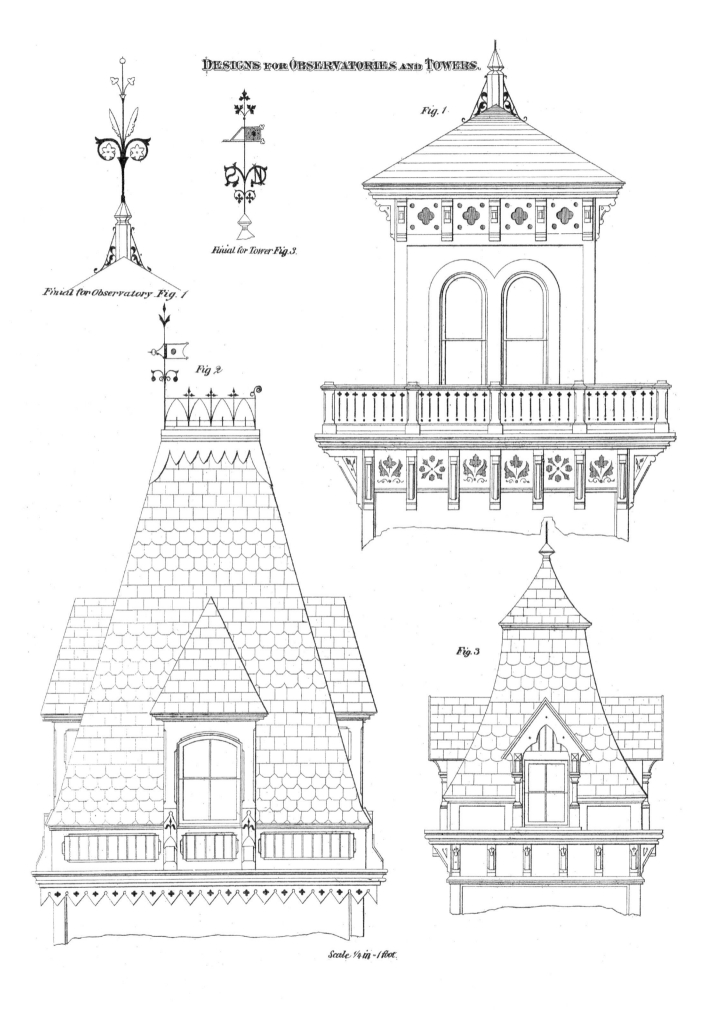

DESIGNS FOR OBSERVATORIES AND TOWERS.

Finial for Tower Fig. 3.

Finial for Observatory Fig. 1.

Fig. 1

Fig. 2

Fig. 3

Scale ¼ in - 1 foot.

PLATE 30

DESIGNS FOR BALCONIES, CANOPIES AND PORCHES.

Scale ¼ inch - one foot.

PLATE 31

PLATE 32

PLATE 33

Plate 34

PLATE 35

FRONT ELEVATION

SIDE ELEVATION

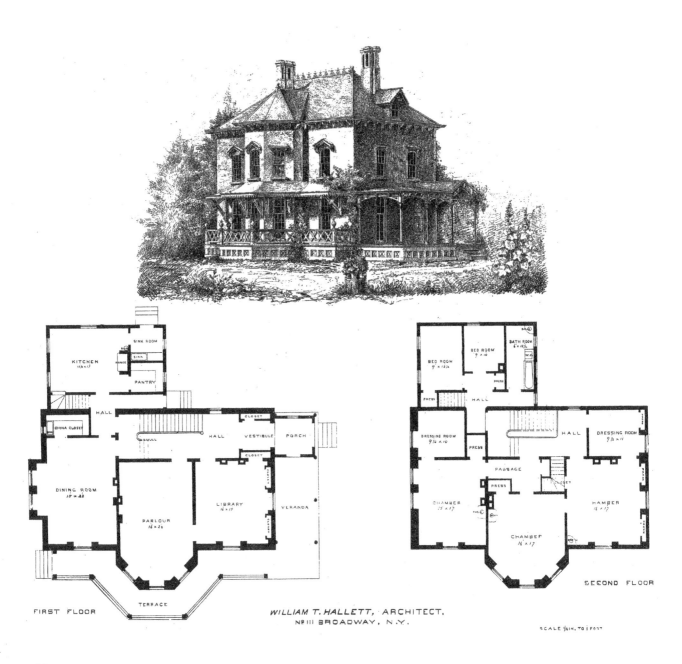

KITCHEN
18 x 17

SINK ROOM

PANTRY

HALL

CHINA CLOSET

HALL

VESTIBULE

PORCH

CLOSET

CLOSET

DINING ROOM
18 x 22

PARLOUR
16 x 24

LIBRARY
16 x 17

VERANDA

FIRST FLOOR

TERRACE

BED ROOM
9 x 13½

BED ROOM
9 x 10

BATH ROOM
6 x 11½

PRESS

HALL

DRESSING ROOM
9½ x 10

PRESS

HALL

DRESSING ROOM
9½ x 11

PASSAGE

PRESS

CLOSET

CHAMBER
15 x 17

CHAMBER
16 x 17

CHAMBER
16 x 17

SECOND FLOOR

WILLIAM T. HALLETT, ARCHITECT.
Nº 111 BROADWAY, N.Y.

SCALE ⅛ IN. TO 1 FOOT

PLATE 36

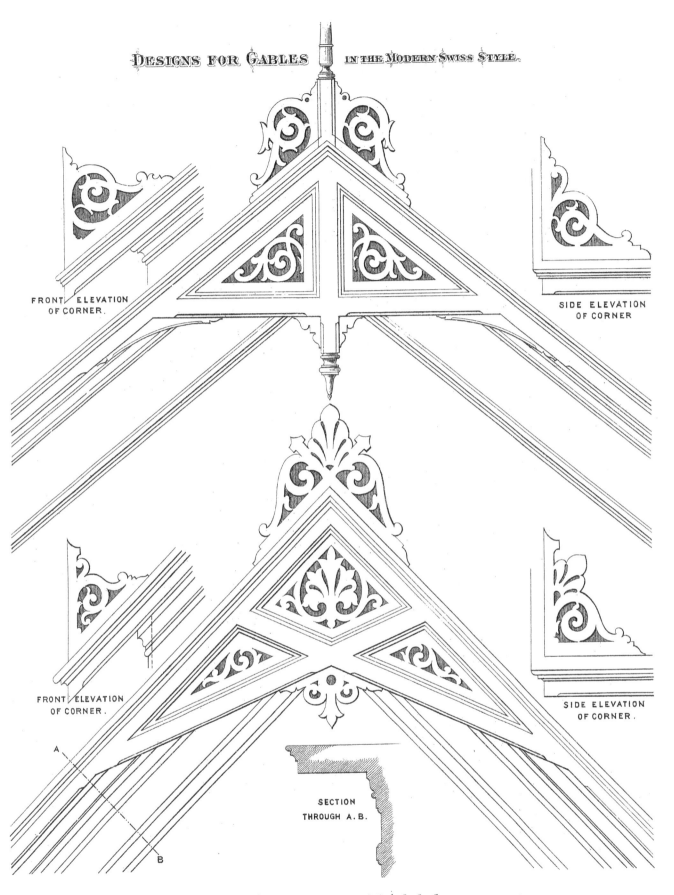

FRONT ELEVATION
OF CORNER.

SIDE ELEVATION
OF CORNER

FRONT ELEVATION
OF CORNER.

SIDE ELEVATION
OF CORNER.

A

B

SECTION
THROUGH A.B.

All sawed work to be of 1½ inch plank.

Scale: ¾ in.=1 ft.

PLATE 37

Scale ¾ in. - 1 foot.

PLATE 38

Designs for Stairs.

SECTION THROUGH HAND RAIL

TREAD

STRING

ELEVATION

GROUNDPLAN.

SECTION THROUGH HAND RAIL

SECTION THROUGH ROSETTE ON POST.

TREAD

STRING

ELEVATION.

GROUNDPLAN.

Scale of Elevations & Groundplans
³/₄ in. = 1 foot.

Scale of Details.
3 in. = 1 foot.

PLATE 39

DESIGNS FOR NEWELS, HAND-RAILS AND BALUSTERS.

Fig. 1.

Fig. 2.

Fig. 3.

Fig. 4.

Fig. 5.

Fig. 6.

Fig. 7.

Fig. 8.

Fig. 9.

Fig. 10.

Fig. 11.

Fig. 12.

Fig. 13.

Fig. 14.

Fig. 15.

Fig. 1. 2. 3. 4. 5. 6. 7. 8. 9. 10. 11. 12.
Scale 1 in. = 1 ft.
Fig. 13. 14. 15.
Scale 1½ in. = 1 ft.

PLATE 40

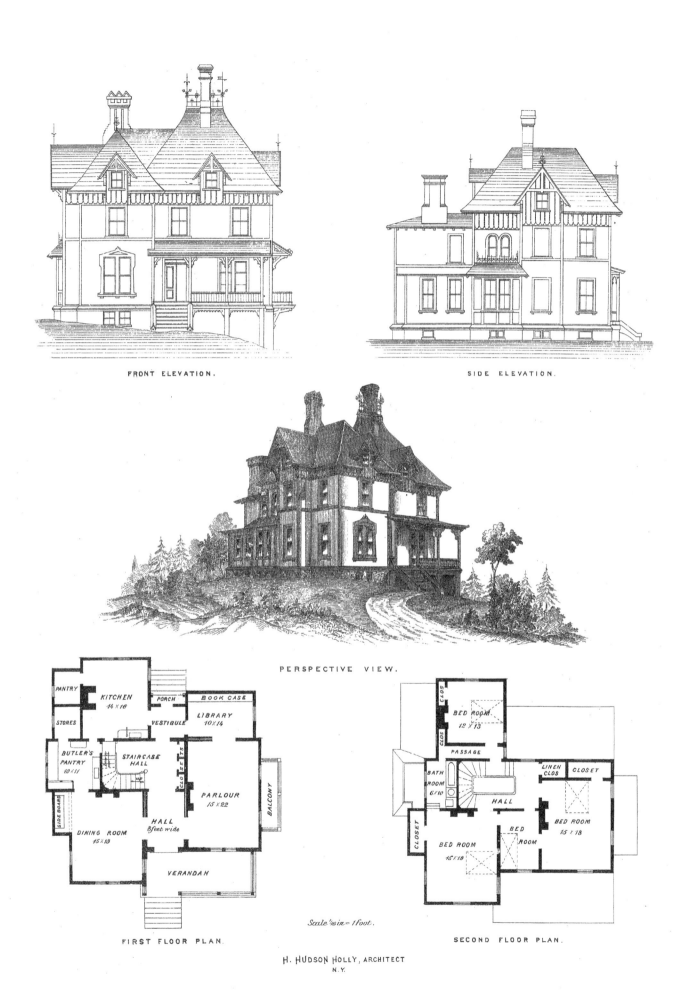

FRONT ELEVATION.

SIDE ELEVATION.

PERSPECTIVE VIEW.

FIRST FLOOR PLAN.

PANTRY

KITCHEN
14 X 16

PORCH

BOOK CASE

STORES

VESTIBULE

LIBRARY
10 X 14

BUTLER'S
PANTRY
10 X 11

STAIRCASE
HALL

CLOSETS

SIDE BOARD

PARLOUR
15 X 22

BALCONY

DINING ROOM
15 X 19

HALL
8 feet wide

VERANDAH

SECOND FLOOR PLAN.

CLOS

BED ROOM
12 X 13

CLOS

PASSAGE

BATH
ROOM
6 X 10

LINEN
CLOS

CLOSET

HALL

CLOSET

BED ROOM
15 X 18

BED ROOM
15 X 18

BED
ROOM

Scale 1/8 in = 1 foot.

H. HUDSON HOLLY, ARCHITECT
N.Y.

PLATE 41

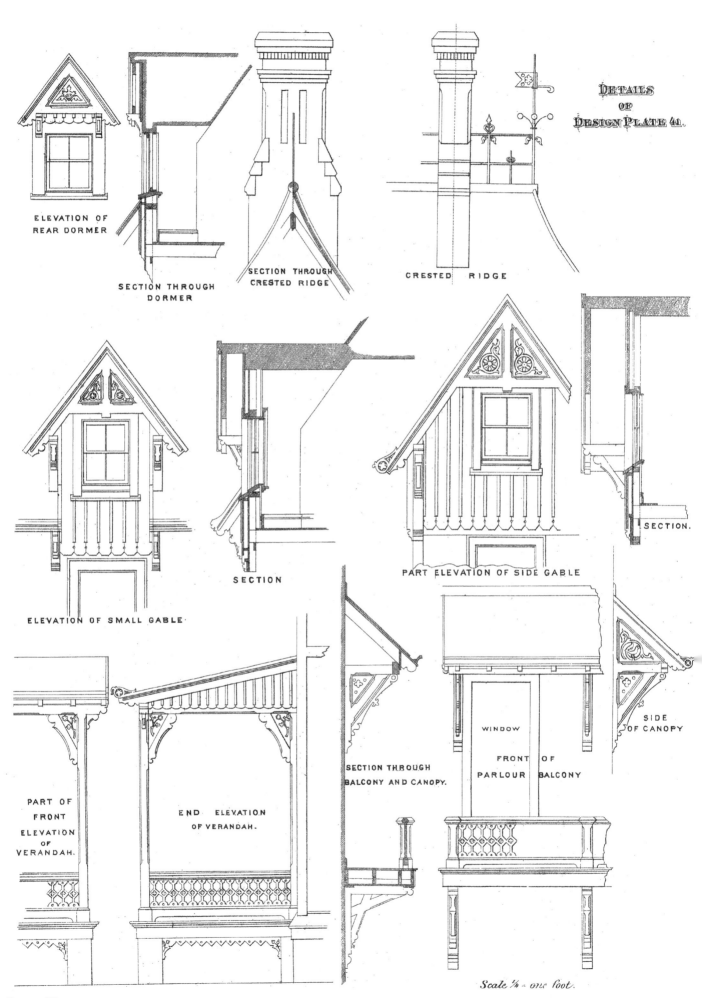

ELEVATION OF
REAR DORMER

SECTION THROUGH
DORMER

SECTION THROUGH
CRESTED RIDGE

CRESTED RIDGE

DETAILS
OF
DESIGN PLATE 41.

ELEVATION OF SMALL GABLE.

SECTION

PART ELEVATION OF SIDE GABLE

SECTION.

PART OF
FRONT
ELEVATION
OF
VERANDAH.

END ELEVATION
OF VERANDAH.

SECTION THROUGH
BALCONY AND CANOPY.

WINDOW

FRONT OF
PARLOUR BALCONY

SIDE
OF CANOPY

Scale ¼ = one foot.

PLATE 42

DESIGNS FOR ARCHITRAVES AND BASE.

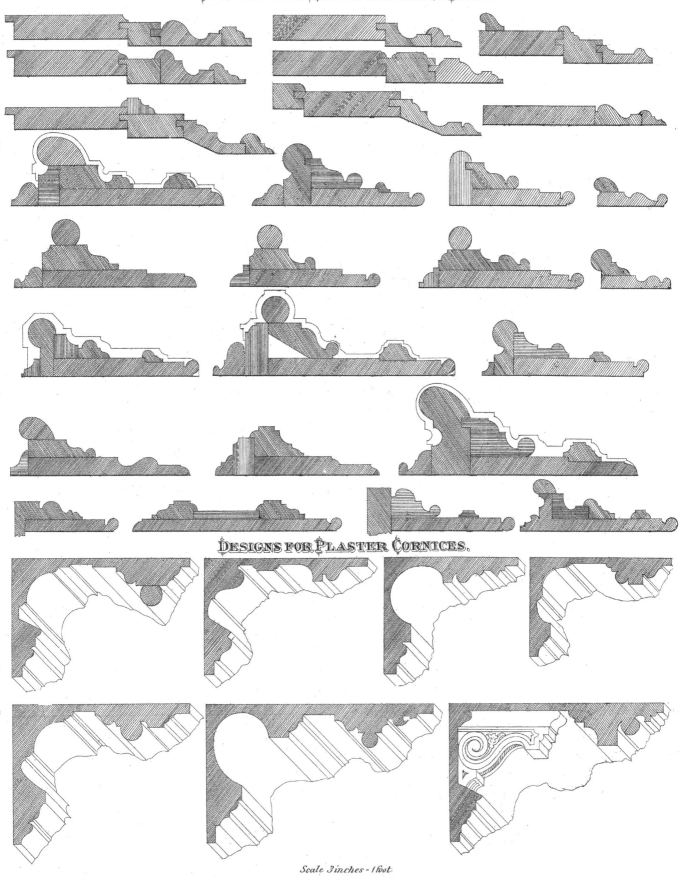

DESIGNS FOR PLASTER CORNICES.

Scale 3 inches = 1 foot

PLATE 43

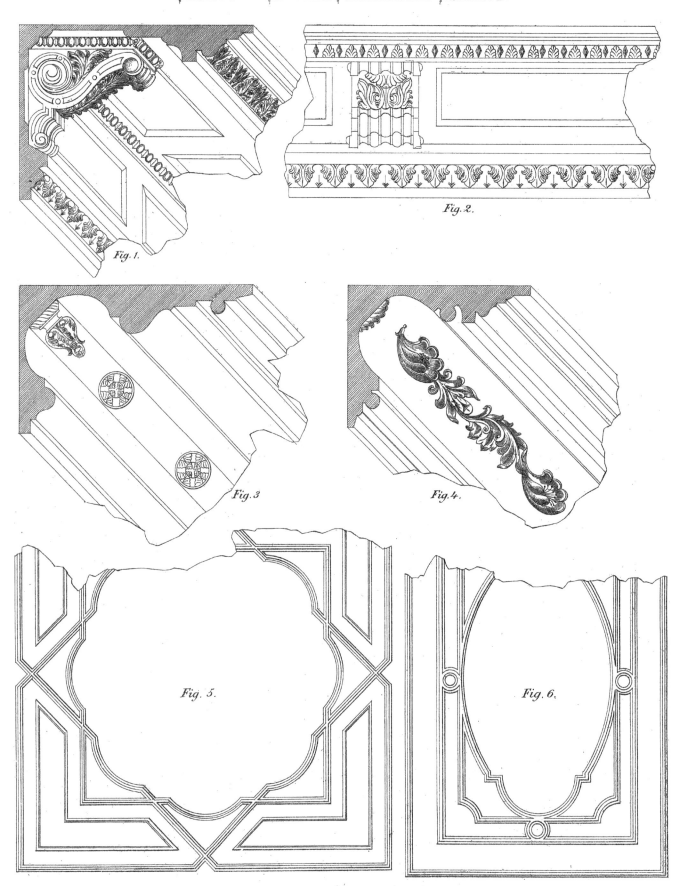

Fig. 1.

Fig. 2.

Fig. 3.

Fig. 4.

Fig. 5.

Fig. 6.

Fig.1,2,3,4, Scale 3in.-1ft., Fig.5.6, ¼in.-1ft.

PLATE 44

Fig. 1

Fig. 2

Fig. 3

Fig. 4

Fig. 5

Fig. 6

Fig. 7

Scale ¾ in - 1 foot

Plate 45

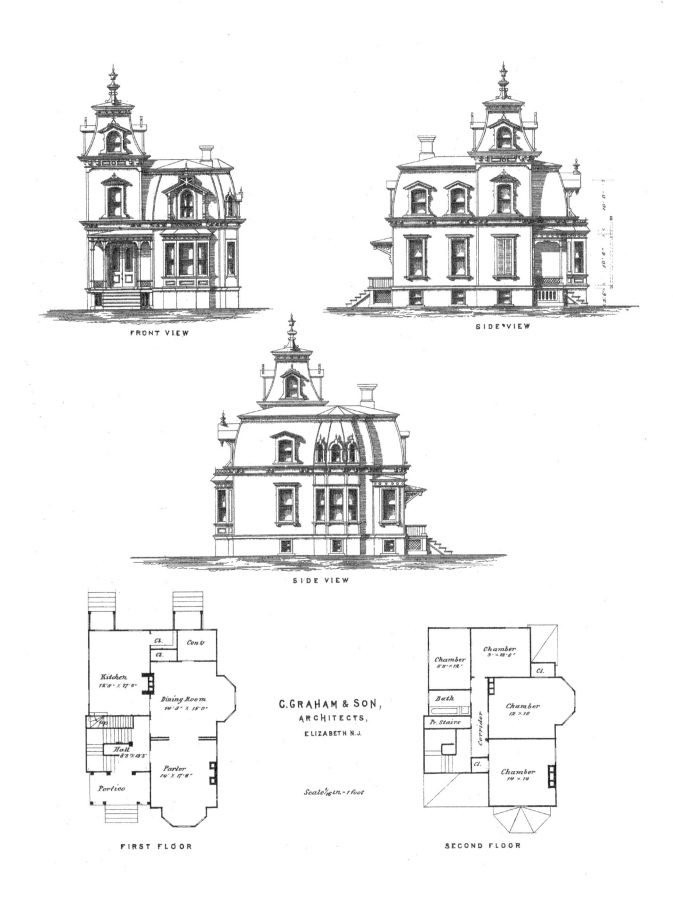

FRONT VIEW

SIDE VIEW

SIDE VIEW

C. GRAHAM & SON,
ARCHITECTS,
ELIZABETH N.J.

Scale 1/16 in. = 1 foot

Kitchen
12'8" x 17'0"

Cl.   Con ty
Cl.

Dining Room
14'8" x 18'0"

Hall
8'2" x 43'3"

Parlor
14' x 17'6"

Portico

FIRST FLOOR

Chamber
8'8" x 12'

Chamber
9' x 13'6"

Cl.

Bath

Pr. Stairs

Corridor

Chamber
12 x 18

Cl.

Chamber
14 x 14

SECOND FLOOR

PLATE 46

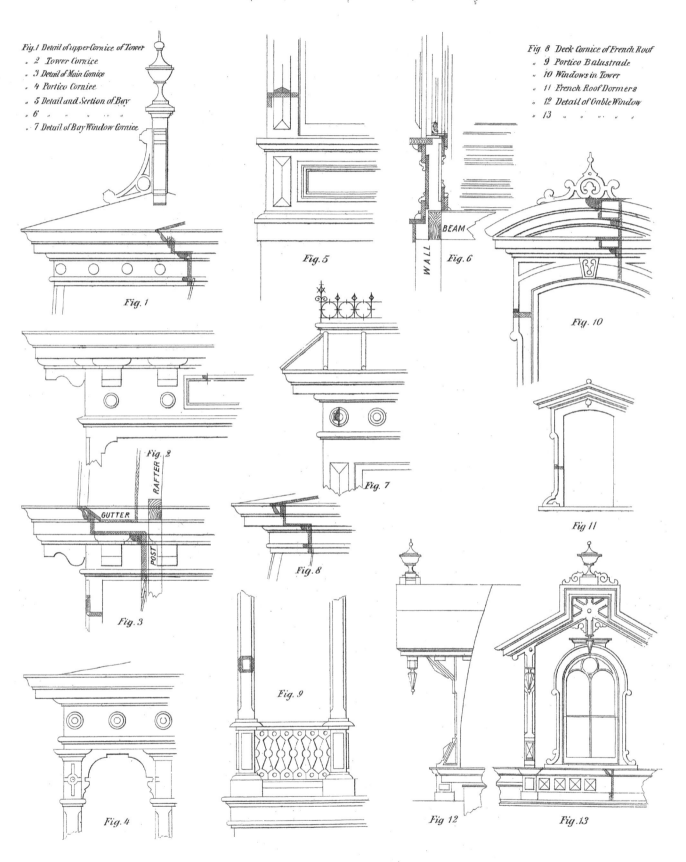

Fig.1 Detail of upper Cornice of Tower
" 2 Tower Cornice
" 3 Detail of Main Cornice
" 4 Portico Cornice
" 5 Detail and Section of Bay
" 6 "
" 7 Detail of Bay Window Cornice

Fig 8 Deck Cornice of French Roof
" 9 Portico Balustrade
" 10 Windows in Tower
" 11 French Roof Dormers
" 12 Detail of Gable Window
" 13 " " " "

Fig. 1

Fig. 5

WALL BEAM Fig. 6

Fig. 10

Fig. 2

RAFTER

GUTTER

POST

Fig. 3

Fig. 7

Fig. 8

Fig 11

Fig. 4

Fig. 9

Fig 12

Fig. 13

DETAILS 1 to 10 are drawn to Scale of ½ in = 1 ft. Fig. 11. 12. 13 ¼ in = 1 ft.

PLATE 47

A.&B. SWISS SUMMER HOUSE. —
Scale ¼ in.= 1 foot.
C.C. ANGLE BRACKETS. D.D. SCROLL BRACKETS, E.E. OPEN PANELS.
Scale 1 in.= 1 foot,
F.F. GABLE ORNAMENTS.— *Scale ½ in.= 1 foot.*

PLATE 48

A AND B. FRONT AND SIDE ELEVATIONS OF SWISS PORCH.

Scale ⅜ in. = 1 Foot.

C. D. E. F. TIMBER BALCONIES. G AND H. SCROLL BRACKETS. I. DROP ORNAMENT.

Scale ½ in. = 1 Foot.

PLATE 49

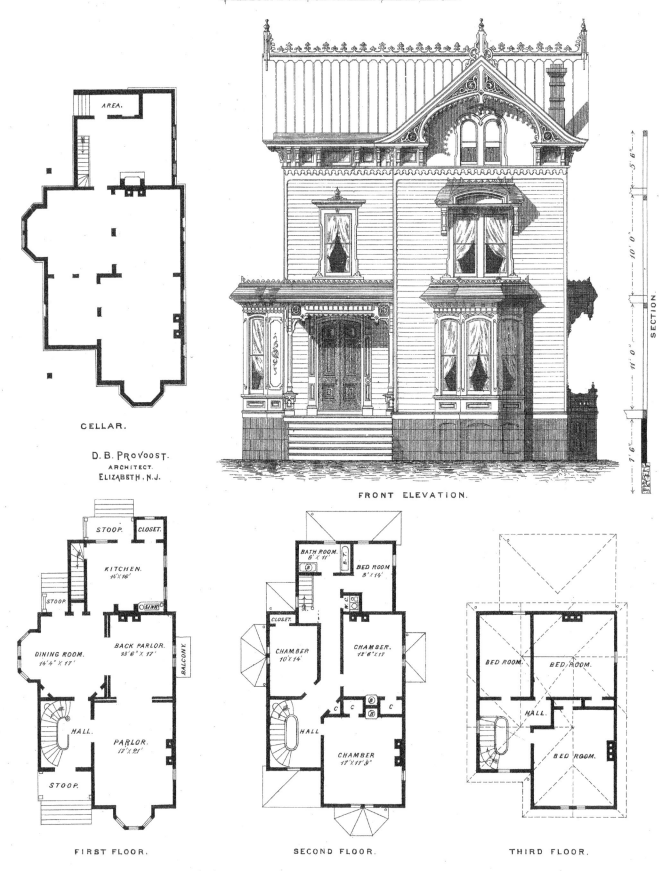

DESIGN FOR SUBURBAN RESIDENCE.

AREA.

CELLAR.

D. B. PROVOOST.
ARCHITECT.
ELIZABETH, N.J.

FRONT ELEVATION.

SECTION.

5' 6" 10' 0" 11' 0" 1' 6"

STOOP. CLOSET.

KITCHEN.
14'x16'

STOOP.

SINK

DINING ROOM.
14'4"x17'

BACK PARLOR.
13'6"x17'

BALCONY

HALL.

PARLOR.
17'x21'

STOOP.

FIRST FLOOR.

BATH ROOM.
6'x11'

B.T.

BED ROOM
8'x14'

W.C.

CLOSET.

CHAMBER
10'x14'

CHAMBER.
12'6"x17'

C C C

HALL.

CHAMBER
17'x17'9"

SECOND FLOOR.

BED ROOM.

BED ROOM.

HALL.

BED ROOM.

THIRD FLOOR.

Scale of Elevation ⅛ inch = one foot, Plans 1/16 inch.

PLATE 50

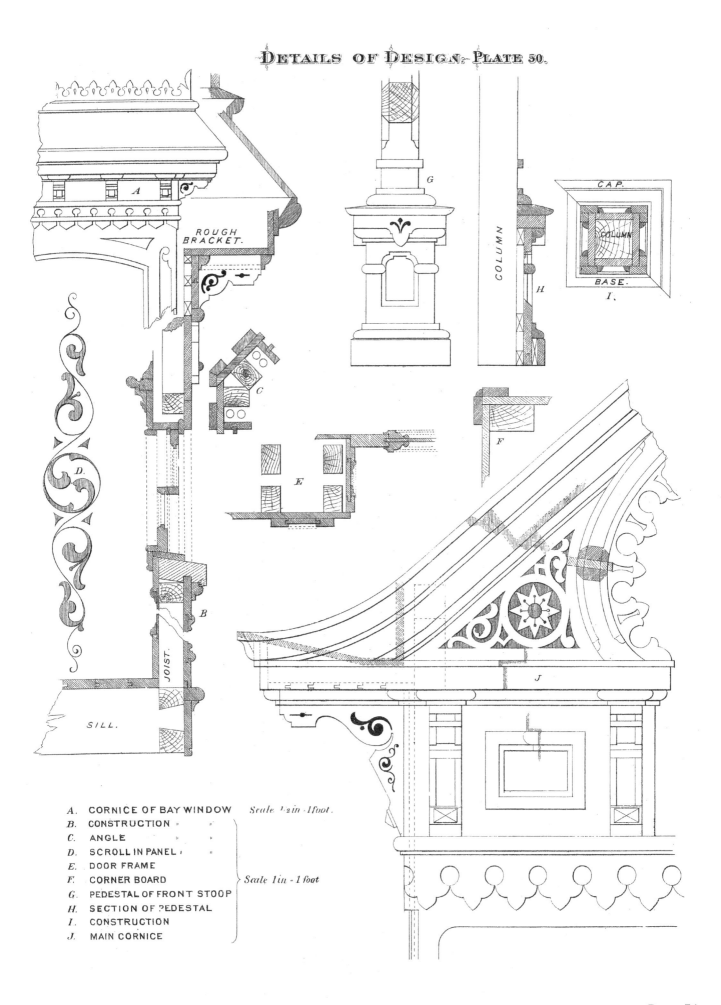

CAP.

COLUMN

BASE.

I.

COLUMN

ROUGH
BRACKET.

A.

C.

D.

B.

E.

F.

G.

H.

J.

JOIST.

SILL.

A. CORNICE OF BAY WINDOW   Scale ¹⁄₂ in - 1 foot.
B. CONSTRUCTION   ,,   ,,
C. ANGLE   ,,   ,,
D. SCROLL IN PANEL   ,,   ,,
E. DOOR FRAME
F. CORNER BOARD   } Scale 1 in - 1 foot
G. PEDESTAL OF FRONT STOOP
H. SECTION OF PEDESTAL
I. CONSTRUCTION
J. MAIN CORNICE

PLATE 51

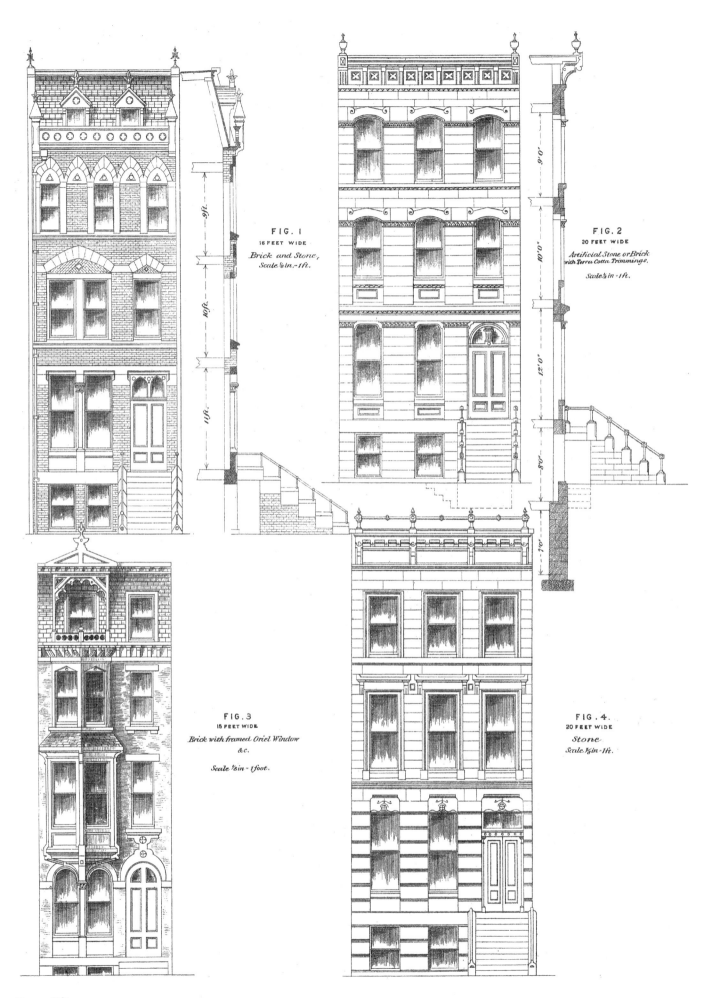

FIG. 1
16 FEET WIDE
Brick and Stone,
Scale ⅛ in.=1 ft.

FIG. 2
20 FEET WIDE
Artificial Stone or Brick
with Terra Cotta Trimmings.
Scale ⅛ in.=1 ft.

FIG. 3
15 FEET WIDE
Brick with framed Oriel Window
&c.
Scale ⅛ in.=1 foot.

FIG. 4.
20 FEET WIDE
Stone
Scale ⅛ in.=1 ft.

PLATE 52

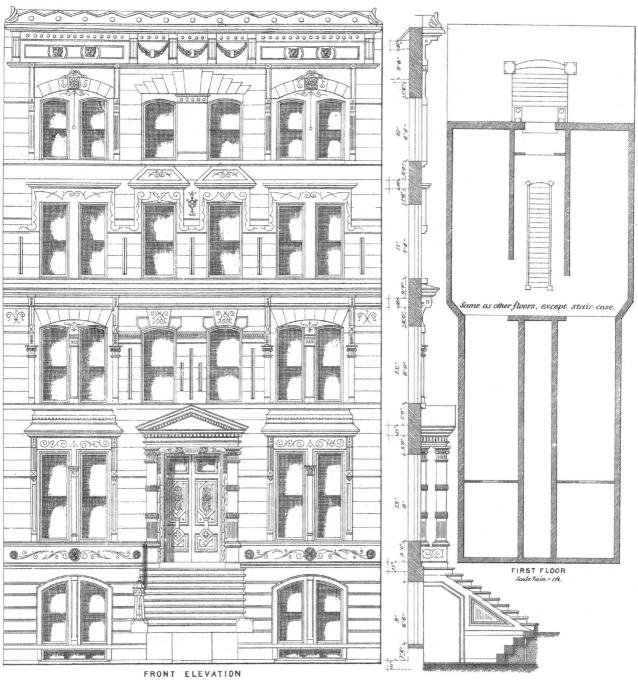

FRONT ELEVATION
Scale 1/8 in.=1 ft.

Same as other floors, except stair-case.

FIRST FLOOR
Scale 1/8 in.=1 ft.

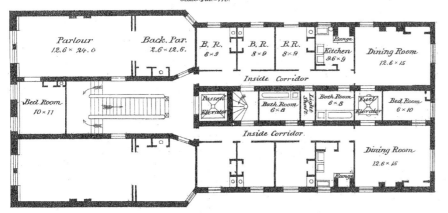

Parlour
12.6 × 24.0

Back. Par.
2.6 × 12.6.

B. R.
6 × 9

B. R.
8 × 9

B. R.
8 × 9

Kitchen
9.6 × 9

Range

Dining Room
12.6 × 15

Inside Corridor

Bed Room
10 × 11

Passen.
Elevator

Light
Shaft

Bath Room
6 × 6

Bath Room
6 × 8

Fuel
Elevator

Bed Room
6 × 10

Inside Corridor.

Dining Room
12.6 × 15

Range

2ND., 3RD., AND 4TH. FLOORS.
Scale 1/8 in.=1 ft.

DESIGN FOR

FRENCH FLAT

WITH ALL IMPROVEMENTS.

Heated by Steam, Hot and Cold Water
furnished by Owner from Boiler in Cellar.

WM. H. CAUVET
ARCHITECT
1497 Broadway, N.Y.

PLATE 53

DESIGN OF HOUSE ARRANGED FOR TWO FAMILIES.

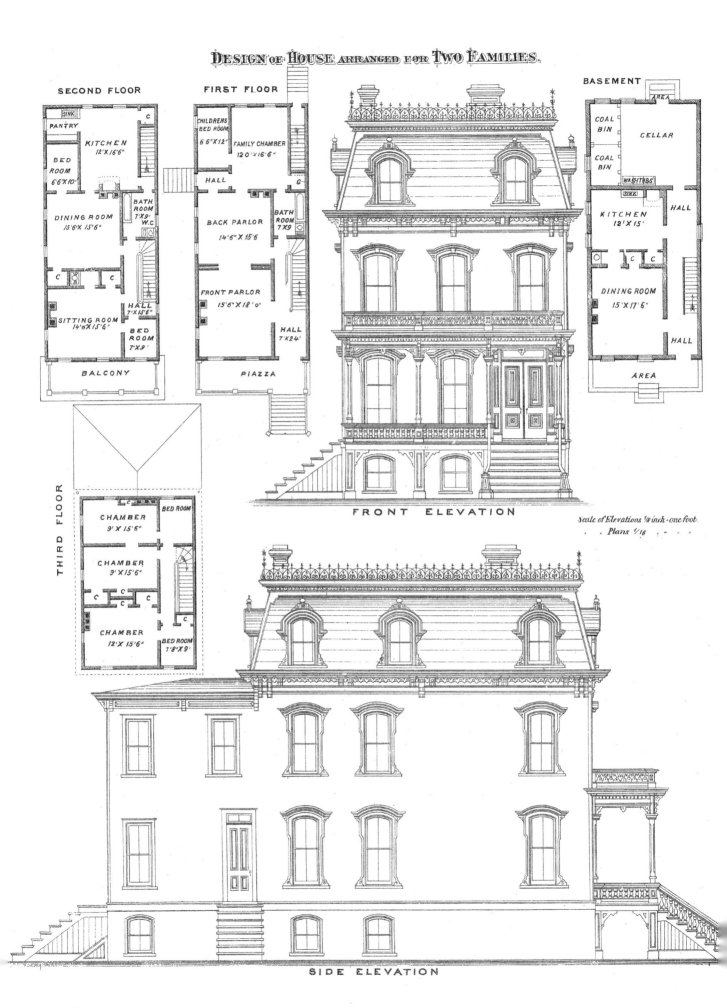

SECOND FLOOR

SINK
PANTRY
KITCHEN 12'X16'6"
C
BED ROOM 6'6"X10'
BATH ROOM 7'X9' W.C.
DINING ROOM 15'6"X15'6"
C
C
ARCH
SITTING ROOM 14'6"X15'6"
HALL 7'X15'6"
BED ROOM 7'X9'
BALCONY

FIRST FLOOR

CHILDRENS BED ROOM 6'6"X12'
FAMILY CHAMBER 12'0"X16'6"
C
HALL
BACK PARLOR 14'6"X15'6"
BATH ROOM 7'X9'
FRONT PARLOR 15'6"X18'0"
HALL 7'X24'
PIAZZA

BASEMENT

AREA
COAL BIN
CELLAR
COAL BIN
WASH TUBS
SINK
KITCHEN 12'X15'
HALL
DINING ROOM 15'X17'6"
C
C
HALL
AREA

THIRD FLOOR

CHAMBER 9'X15'6"
BED ROOM
CHAMBER 9'X15'6"
C
C
CHAMBER 12'X15'6"
BED ROOM 7'8"X9'

FRONT ELEVATION

Scale of Elevations ⅛ inch - one foot.
Plans 1/16

SIDE ELEVATION

PLATE 54

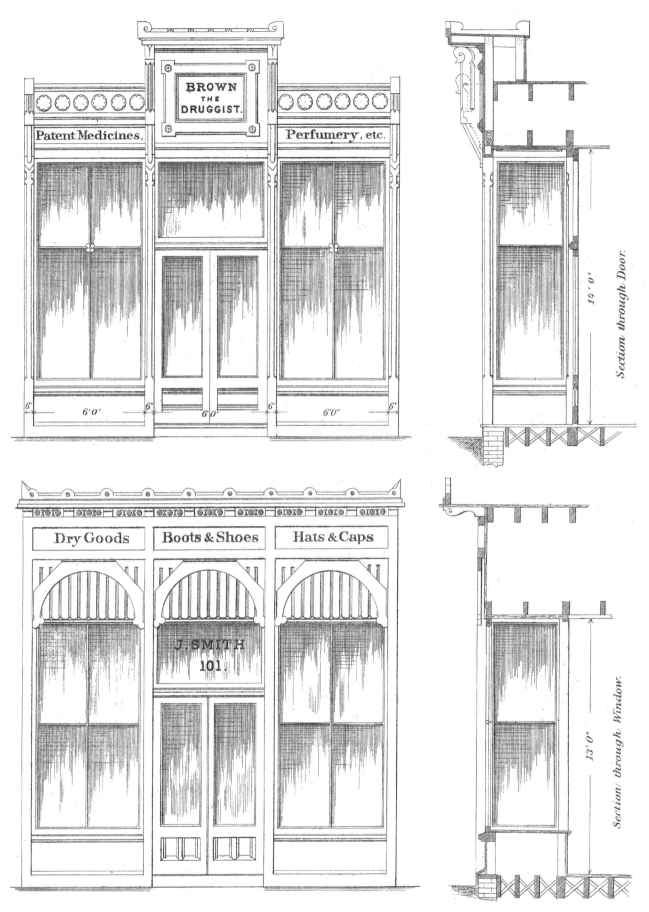

BROWN
THE
DRUGGIST.

Patent Medicines,   Perfumery, etc.

6"   6'0"   6"   6'0"   6"   6'0"   6"

Section through Door.

14'0"

Dry Goods   Boots & Shoes   Hats & Caps

J. SMITH
101.

Section through Window.

13'0"

TWO ONE-STORY STORE FRONTS.

Scale ¼ in = 1 ft.

PLATE 55

DESIGNS FOR STORE FRONTS.

A.

B.

C.

D.

E.

Fig. 1.

Fig. 2.

Fig. 3.

Fig 1. DESIGN OF STORE, 22 FEET FRONT   Scale ¼ in - 1 foot.
Fig. 2.   ..   .   ..   17 ½   ..   Scale ¼ in - 1 foot.
Fig. 3.   ..   .   ..   14 ½   ..   Scale ¼ in - 1 foot.
A. DESIGN OF MAIN CORNICE for Fig.1. Scale ½ in - 1 foot.
B.& C. DETAILS   .   ..   .   Scale ¾ in - 1 foot.
D.& E.   ..   .   FRONT   ..   .   Scale ¾ in - 1 foot.

PLATE 56

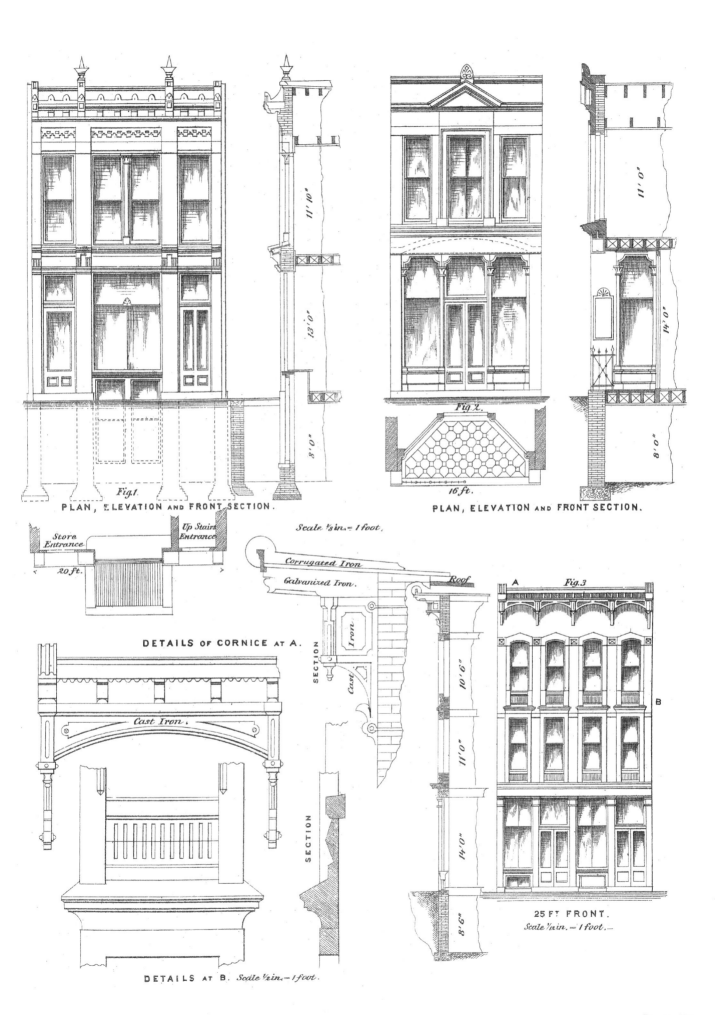

PLAN, ELEVATION AND FRONT SECTION.

Fig.1.

11' 10"

13' 0"

8' 0"

PLAN, ELEVATION AND FRONT SECTION.

Fig. 2.

11' 0"

14' 0"

8' 0"

16 ft.

Store Entrance

Up Stairs Entrance

20 ft.

Scale ½ in. = 1 foot.

Corrugated Iron

Galvanized Iron.

Roof

DETAILS OF CORNICE AT A.

Cast Iron.

SECTION

Iron.

Cast

SECTION

DETAILS AT B. *Scale ½ in. = 1 foot.*

A

Fig. 3.

B

10' 6"

11' 0"

14' 0"

8' 6"

25 FT FRONT.

Scale ½ in. = 1 foot.

PLATE 57

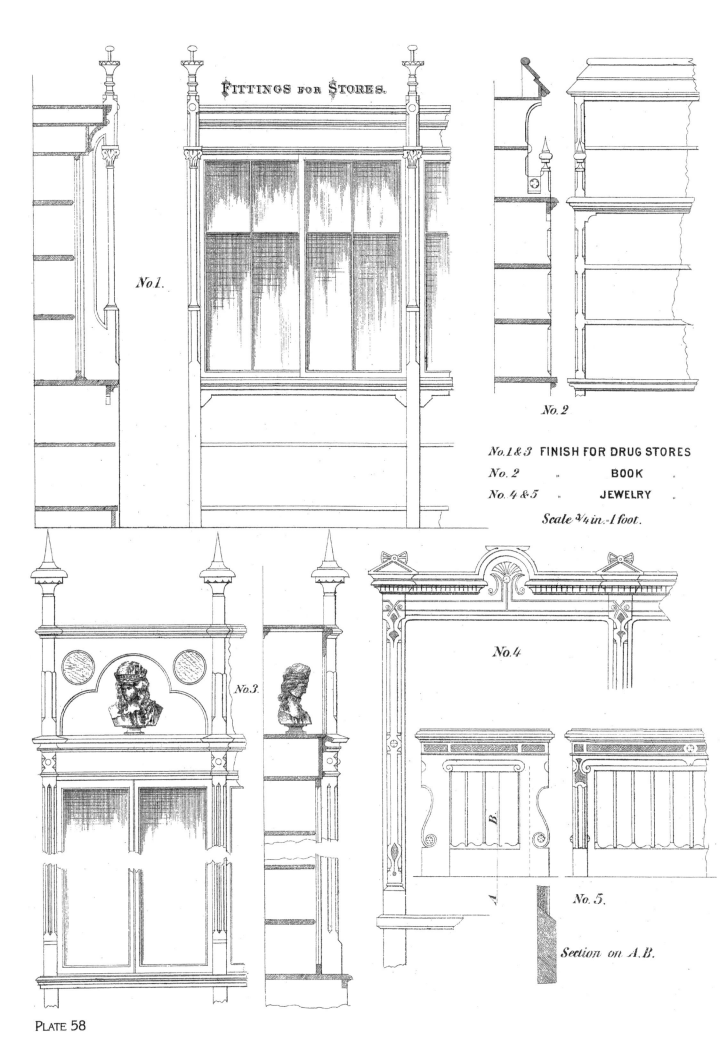

FITTINGS FOR STORES.

No.1.

No. 2

No.1 & 3 FINISH FOR DRUG STORES
No. 2 " BOOK "
No. 4 & 5 " JEWELRY "

Scale ¼ in.= 1 foot.

No.3.

No.4

B.

A.

No. 5.

Section on A.B.

PLATE 58

FITTINGS FOR STORES.

No. 1.

No. 2.

No. 3.

No. 4.

No. 5.

No. 1 & 2 SHELVING for DRY GOODS STORES.
„   3 COUNTER   „   „   „
„   4 FINISH for FURNISHING GOODS.
„   5   „   „   DRUG or FANCY STORE.
Scale: 1, 2, 3 & 4: ¾ in.—1 foot; 5: ½ in.—1 foot.

PLATE 59

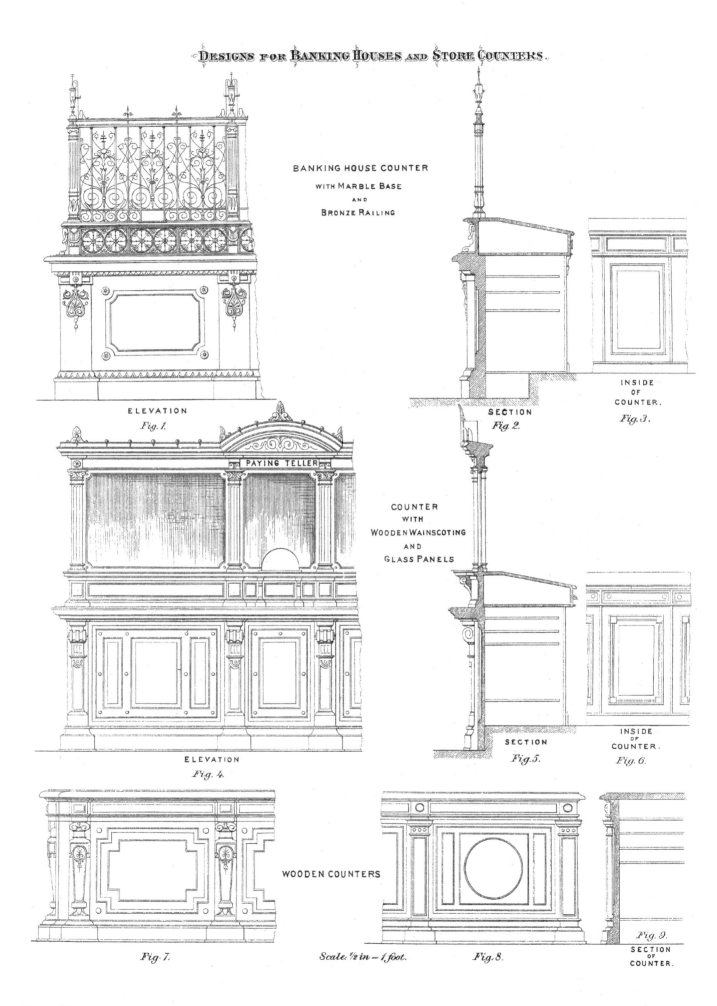

BANKING HOUSE COUNTER
WITH MARBLE BASE
AND
BRONZE RAILING

ELEVATION
Fig. 1.

SECTION
Fig. 2.

INSIDE
OF
COUNTER.
Fig. 3.

PAYING TELLER

COUNTER
WITH
WOODEN WAINSCOTING
AND
GLASS PANELS

ELEVATION
Fig. 4.

SECTION
Fig. 5.

INSIDE
OF
COUNTER.
Fig. 6.

WOODEN COUNTERS

Fig. 7.

Scale: ½ in = 1 foot.

Fig. 8.

Fig. 9.
SECTION
OF
COUNTER.

PLATE 60

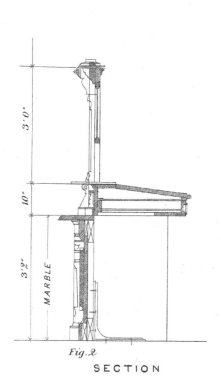

Fig. 2
SECTION

3'-0"

10"

3'-2"

MARBLE

Fig. 1
ELEVATION

DIVIDENDS

Edwᴰ H. Kendall
ARCHITECT.
No. 120 Broadway.
N. Y.

3'-8"
GLASS
SHELF

4"   4"

Fig. 3
PLAN

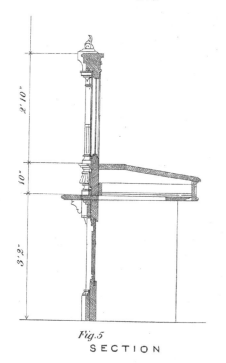

Fig. 5
SECTION

2'-10"

10"

3'-2"

DISCOUNTS

Fig. 4
ELEVATION

Scale ½ in. = 1 foot

Plate 61

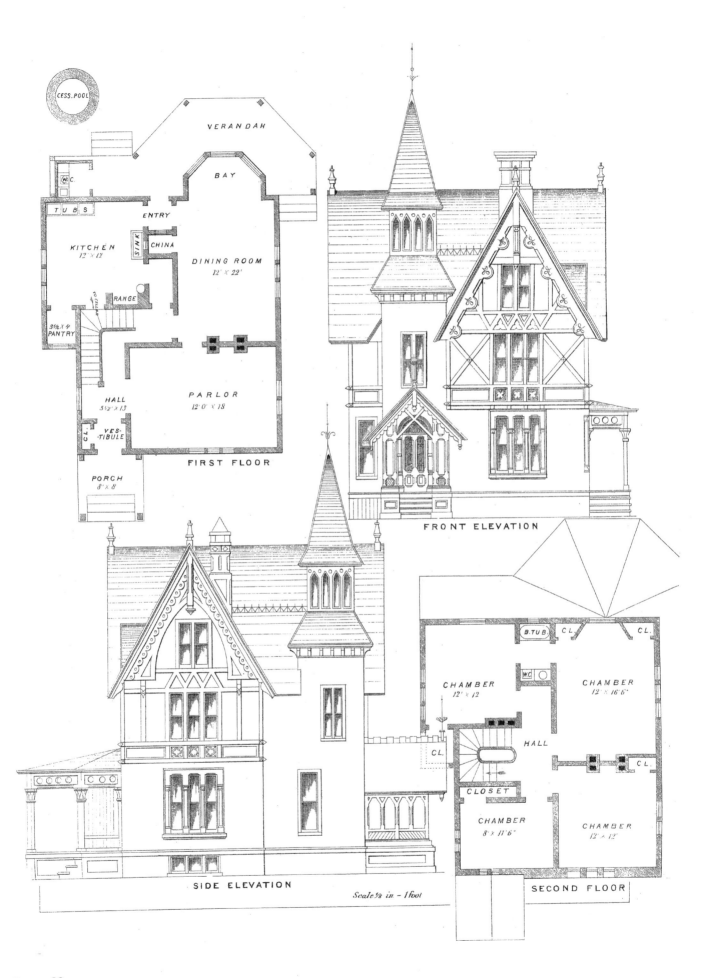

CESS.POOL

VERANDAH

BAY

W.C.

T U B S

ENTRY

KITCHEN
12' x 12

SINK

CHINA

DINING ROOM
12' x 22'

RANGE

TO CELLAR

3½ x 4
PANTRY

PARLOR
12'0" x 18

C.L.

HALL
5½' x 13

VES-
TIBULE

FIRST FLOOR

PORCH
8' x 8

FRONT ELEVATION

SIDE ELEVATION

Scale ½ in = 1 foot

B.TUB

CL.

CL.

CHAMBER
12' x 12

W.C.

CHAMBER
12' x 16'6"

CL.

HALL

CLOSET

CL.

CHAMBER
8' x 11'6"

CHAMBER
12' x 12

SECOND FLOOR

PLATE 62

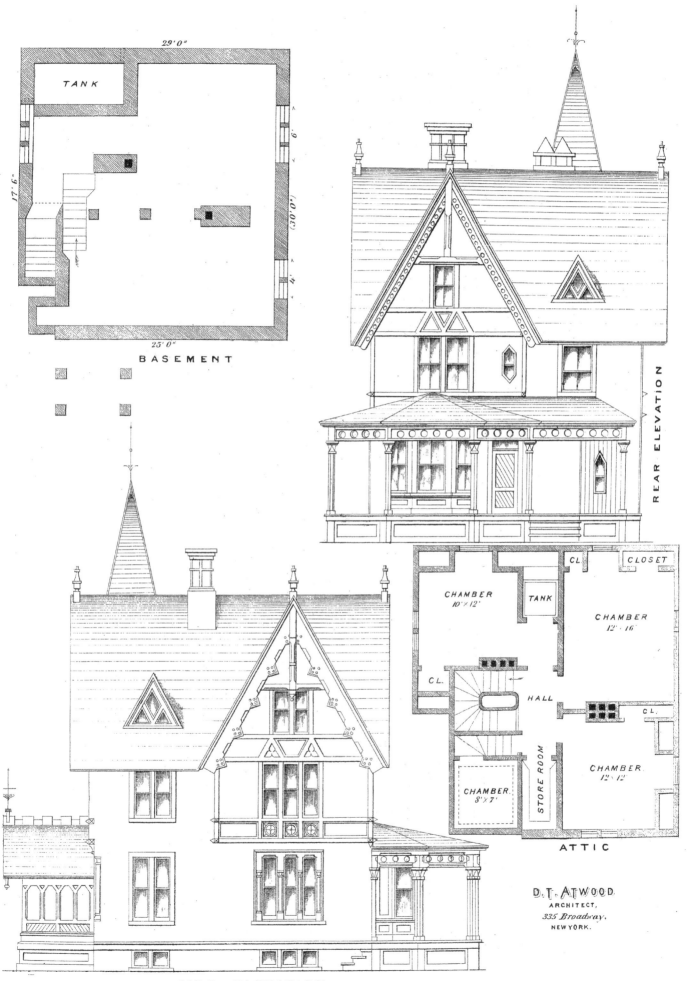

29' 0"

TANK

17' 6"

(30' 0")

25' 0"

BASEMENT

REAR ELEVATION

CLOSET
C.L.

CHAMBER
10' × 12'

TANK

CHAMBER
12' × 16'

C.L.

HALL

CL.

CHAMBER
8' × 7'

STORE ROOM

CHAMBER
12' × 12'

ATTIC

D. T. ATWOOD
ARCHITECT,
335 Broadway,
NEW YORK.

SIDE ELEVATION

PLATE 63

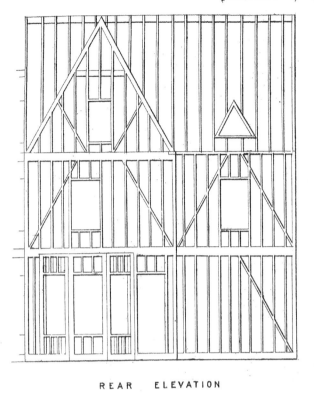

REAR ELEVATION

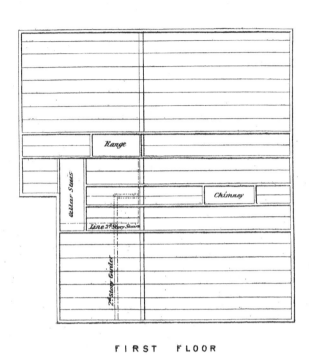

FIRST FLOOR

FRONT ELEVATION   Scale ⅛ inch - 1 foot.   SIDE ELEVATION

PLATE 64

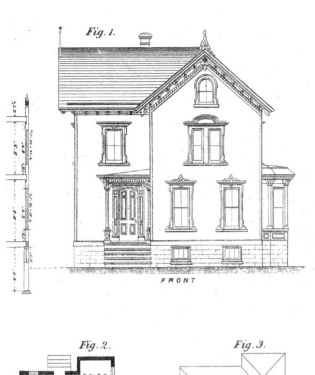

Fig. 1.

FRONT

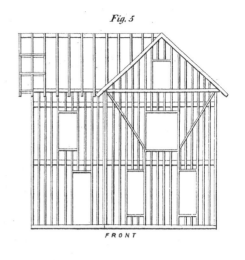

Fig. 5

FRONT

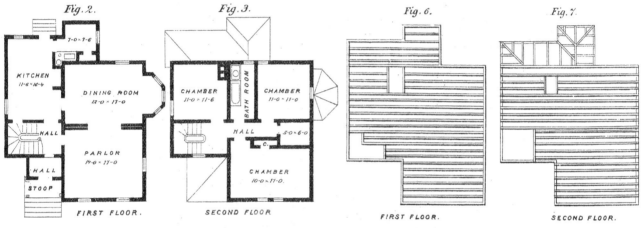

Fig. 2.

KITCHEN
11·6×16·4

DINING ROOM
12·0×11·0

HALL

HALL

STOOP

PARLOR
14·0×11·0

7·0×7·6

FIRST FLOOR.

Fig. 3.

CHAMBER
11·0×11·6

BATH ROOM

CHAMBER
11·0×11·0

HALL

5·0×6·0

C.

CHAMBER
10·0×11·0

SECOND FLOOR

Fig. 6.

FIRST FLOOR.

Fig. 7.

SECOND FLOOR.

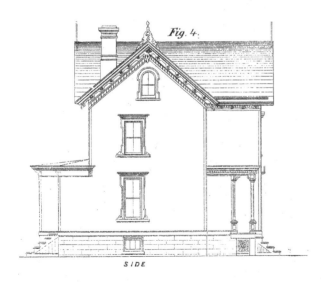

Fig. 4.

SIDE

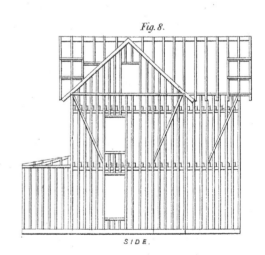

Fig. 8.

SIDE.

Fig.1. Front Elevation   Fig.3. Second Floor   Fig. 5 Framing of Front   Fig.7. Framing of Second Floor
" 2. First Floor   " 4. Side Elevation   " 6.   "   " First Floor   " 8   "   " Side Elevation.

Fig. 2. 3. 4. & 7 Scale 1/16 in. = 1 foot.

PLATE 65

BALLOON FRAME FOR SMALL COTTAGE.

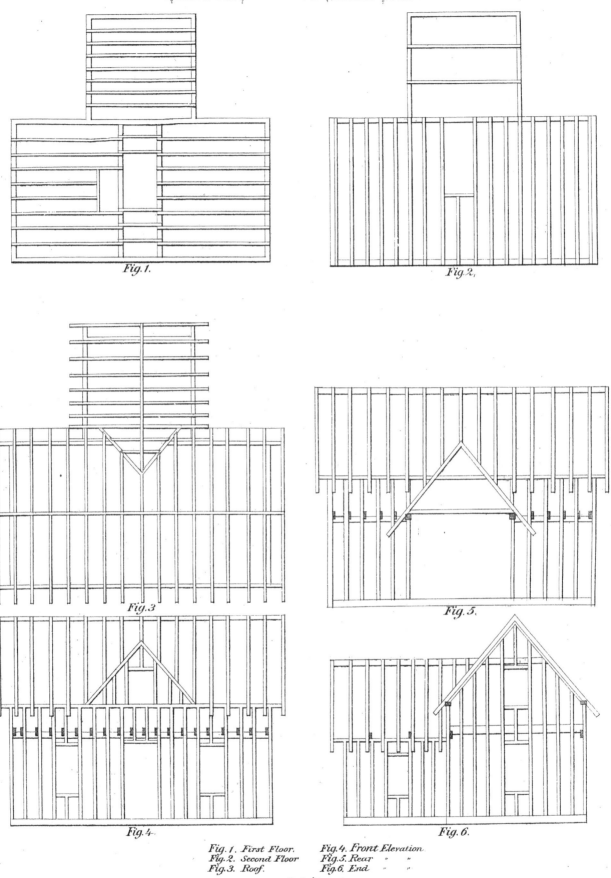

Fig.1.

Fig.2.

Fig.3.

Fig.4.

Fig.5.

Fig.6.

Fig.1. First Floor. Fig.4. Front Elevation.
Fig.2. Second Floor Fig.5. Rear   "   "
Fig.3. Roof. Fig.6. End   "   "

Scale ⅛ in.- 1 ft.

PLATE 66

FRAME FOR GOTHIC RESIDENCE.

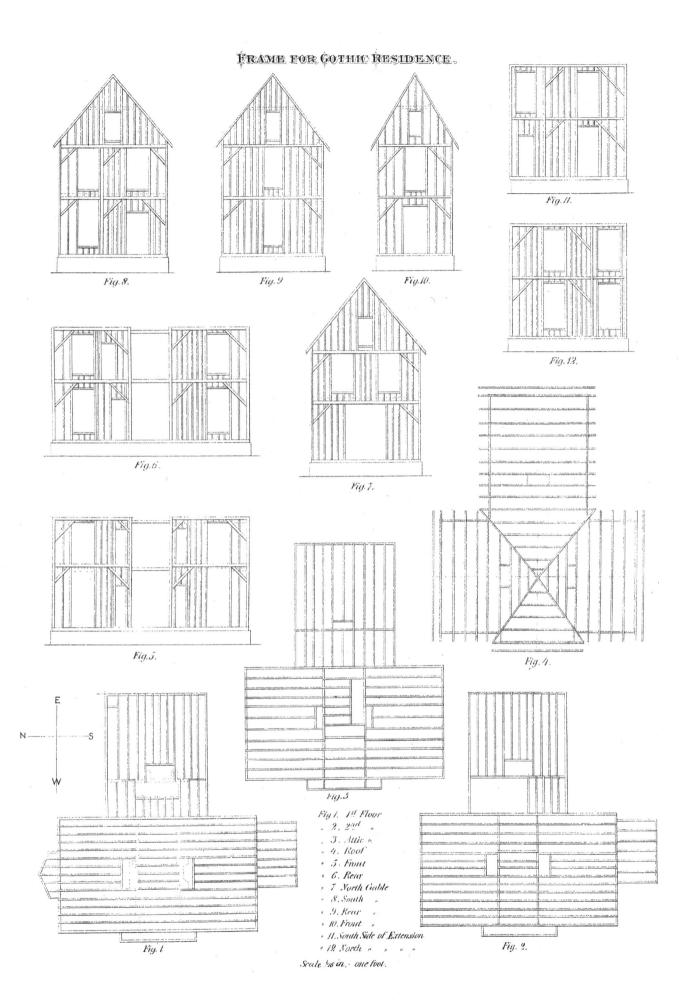

Fig. 8.

Fig. 9.

Fig. 10.

Fig. 11.

Fig. 12.

Fig. 6.

Fig. 7.

Fig. 5.

Fig. 4.

E

N — S

W

Fig. 3.

Fig 1. 1st Floor
„ 2. 2nd „
„ 3. Attic „
„ 4. Roof
„ 5. Front
„ 6. Rear
„ 7. North Gable
„ 8. South „
„ 9. Rear „
„ 10. Front „
„ 11. South Side of Extension
„ 12. North „ „ „

Fig. 1.

Fig. 2.

Scale ⅛ in. — one foot.

PLATE 67

FRAME FOR SMALL DOUBLE HOUSE WITH MANSARD ROOF.

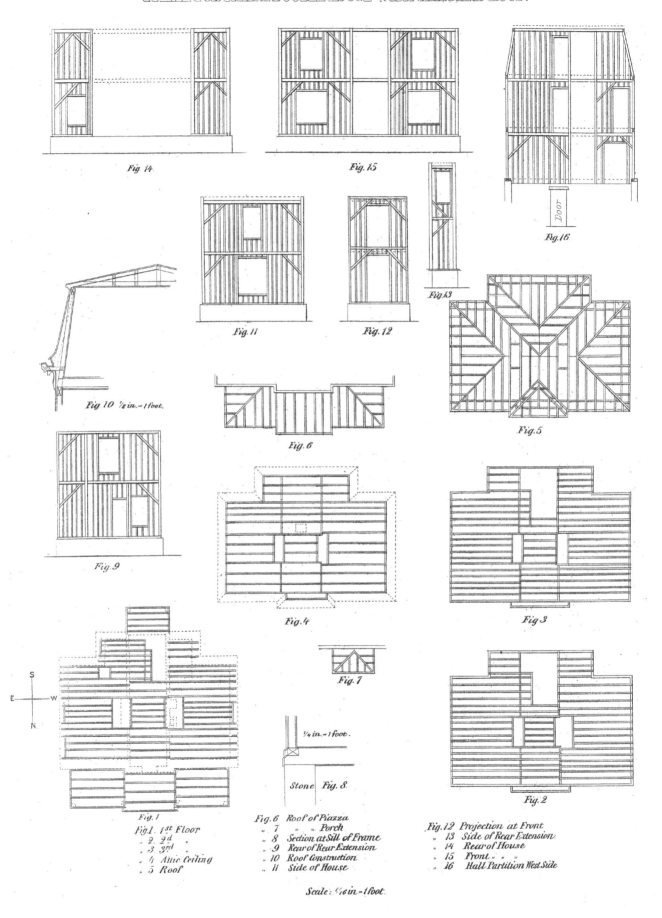

Fig. 14.

Fig. 15.

Fig. 16.

Fig. 13.

Fig. 11.

Fig. 12.

Fig. 10. ⅛ in. = 1 foot.

Fig. 5.

Fig. 6.

Fig. 9.

Fig. 4.

Fig 3.

Fig. 7.

¼ in. = 1 foot.

Stone | Fig. 8.

Fig. 1.

Fig.1. 1st Floor
" 2. 2d "
" 3. 3rd "
" 4. Attic Ceiling
" 5. Roof

Fig. 6. Roof of Piazza
" 7. " " Porch
" 8. Section at Sill of Frame
" 9. Rear of Rear Extension
" 10. Roof Construction
" 11. Side of House

Fig. 12. Projection at Front
" 13. Side of Rear Extension
" 14. Rear of House
" 15. Front " "
" 16. Hall Partition West Side

Scale: ¹⁄₁₆ in = 1 foot.

PLATE 68

FRAME OF A SIDE HILL BARN.

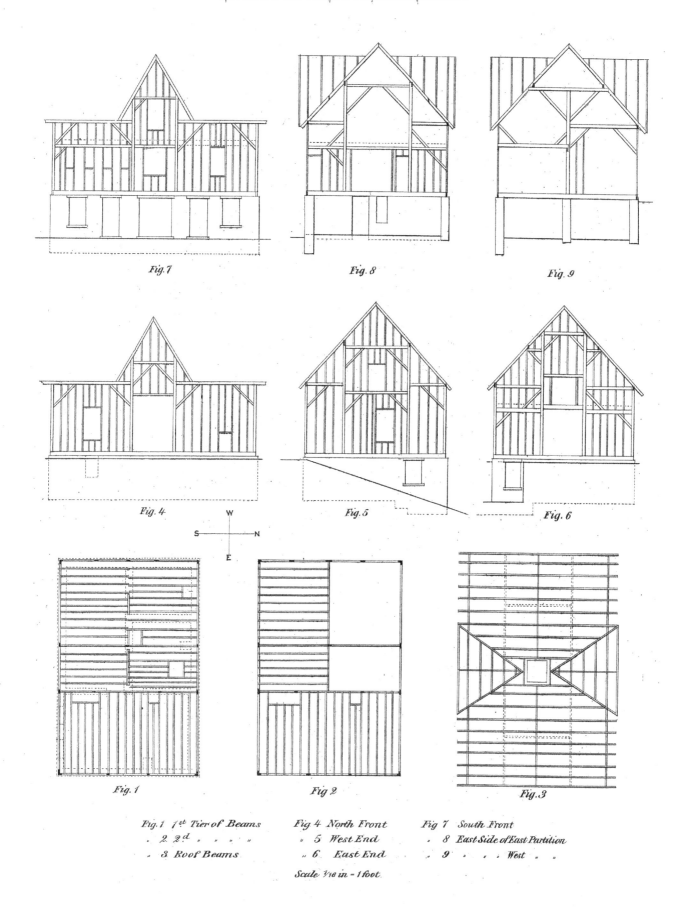

Fig. 7   Fig. 8   Fig. 9

Fig. 4   Fig. 5   Fig. 6

W · S · N · E

Fig. 1   Fig. 2   Fig. 3

Fig. 1 1st Tier of Beams   Fig 4 North Front   Fig 7 South Front
  „ 2 2d „ „ „   „ 5 West End   „ 8 East Side of East Partition
  „ 3 Roof Beams   „ 6 East End   „ 9 „ „ „ West „ „

Scale 3/16 in = 1 foot.

PLATE 69

FRAME FOR A LARGE BARN.

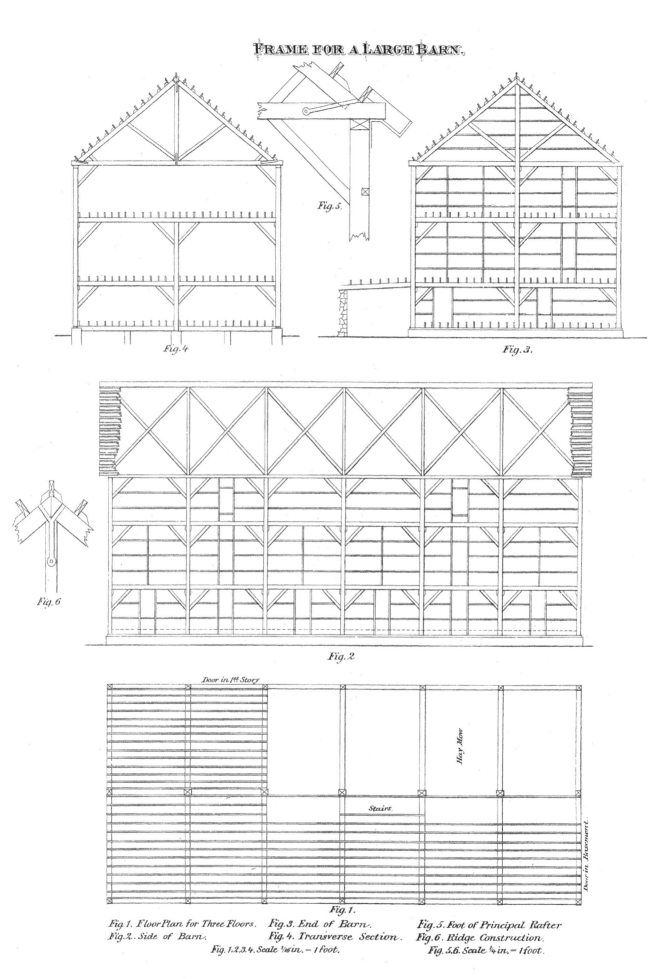

Fig. 5.

Fig. 4.

Fig. 3.

Fig. 6

Door in 1st Story

Hay Mow

Stairs.

Door in Basement.

Fig. 2.

Fig. 1.

Fig. 1. Floor Plan for Three Floors.   Fig. 3. End of Barn.   Fig. 5. Foot of Principal Rafter

Fig. 2. Side of Barn.   Fig. 4. Transverse Section.   Fig. 6. Ridge Construction.

Fig. 1, 2, 3, 4. Scale 1/16 in. = 1 foot.   Fig. 5, 6. Scale 1/4 in. = 1 foot.

PLATE 70

FRAME FOR EXHIBITION BUILDINGS.

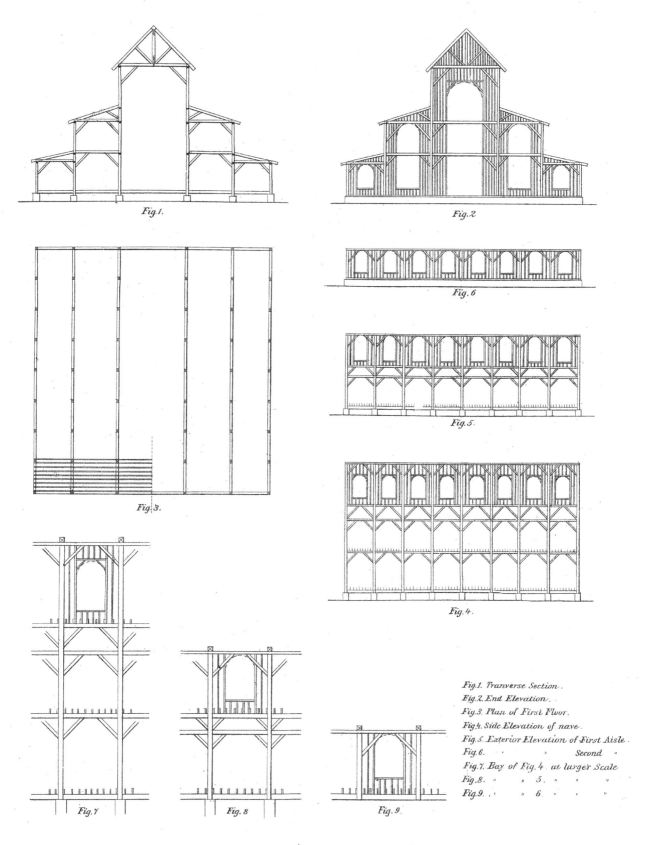

Fig.1.

Fig.2

Fig.6

Fig.5.

Fig.4.

Fig.3.

Fig.7

Fig.8

Fig.9.

Fig.1. Transverse Section.
Fig.2. End Elevation.
Fig.3. Plan of First Floor.
Fig.4. Side Elevation of nave.
Fig.5. Exterior Elevation of First Aisle.
Fig.6. "   "   Second "
Fig.7. Bay of Fig.4. at larger Scale
Fig.8. "   "   5. "   "   "
Fig.9. "   "   6 "   "   "

Scale ⅟₃₂ in. = 1 foot.
Details ⅟₁₆ in. = 1 foot.

PLATE 71

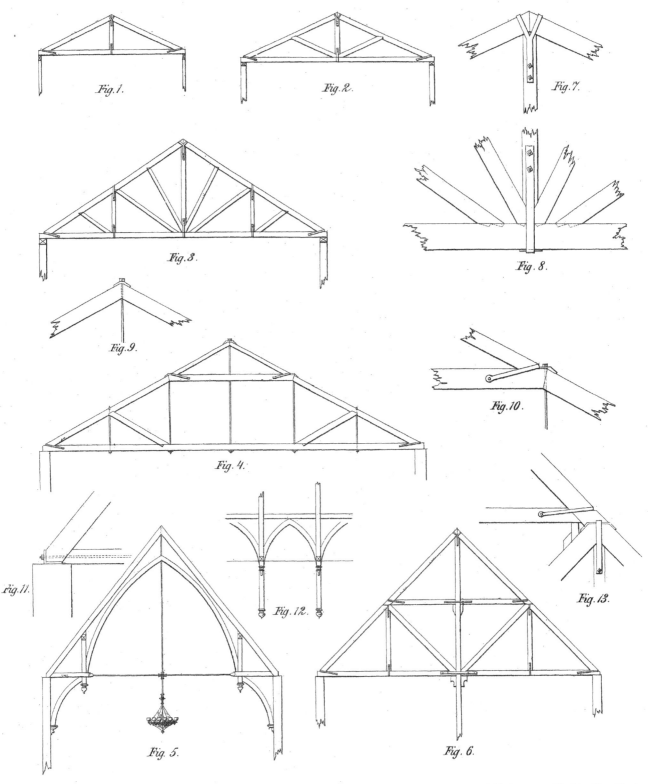

Fig. 1.

Fig. 2.

Fig. 7.

Fig. 3.

Fig. 8.

Fig. 9.

Fig. 10.

Fig. 4.

Fig. 11.

Fig. 12.

Fig. 13.

Fig. 5.

Fig. 6.

Fig. 1. Roof Truss of 30 ft. Span.
Fig. 2. Roof Truss of 40 ft. Span.
Fig. 3. Roof Truss of 60 ft. Span.
Fig. 4. Roof Truss of 80 ft. Span.
Fig. 5. Church Roof of 50 ft. Span.
Fig. 6. Warehouse Roof of 60 ft. Span.
Fig. 7. Connection at Ridge of Fig. 1, 2, 3, 6.
Fig. 8. Connection of King Post of Fig. 3.
Fig. 9. Ridge of Fig. 4.
Fig. 10. Connection of Straining Piece, Fig. 4.
Fig. 11. Foot of Rafter Fig. 5.
Fig. 12. One Bay of Roof of Fig. 5.
Fig. 13. Connection of Straining Piece at Fig. 6.

Scale ⅟₁₆ in. = 1 foot.
Details ¼ in. = 1 foot.

Plate 72

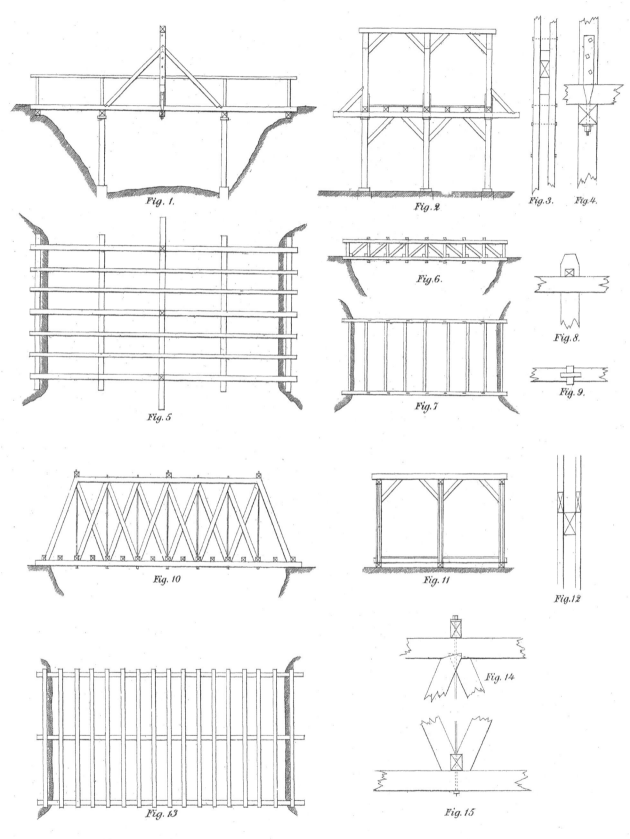

Fig. 1.

Fig. 2.

Fig. 3.   Fig. 4.

Fig. 5

Fig. 6.

Fig. 7

Fig. 8.

Fig. 9.

Fig. 10

Fig. 11

Fig.12

Fig. 14

Fig. 15

Fig. 13

Fig 1	Bridge over a Road	Fig 4	Connection at Tie Beam	Fig. 7	Plan of Fig. 6	Fig. 10	Strong Bridge of 50ft. span	Fig. 13	Plan of Fig. 10
„ 2	Section of same	„ 5	Plan of Fig. 1	„ 8	Side Elevation of Ties at Top	„ 11	Section of same	„ 14	Connection at Top
„ 3	Construction of Post.	„ 6	Light Bridge of 30 ft. span.	„ 9	Top View of Ties	„ 12	Arrangement of Braces.	„ 15	„ „ „ Bottom.

Scale ¼ in = 1 foot. Details ½ inch.

Plate 73

DESIGNS FOR COTTAGES AND VILLAS.

Fig. 1.

Fig. 2.

Fig. 3.

Fig. 4.

Fig. 5.

Fig. 6.

Fig. 7.

Fig. 8.

Fig. 9.

1, 4, 5, 6, 7, 8 & 9: Scale ⅛ in. – 1 foot. _ 2 & 3: Scale ³⁄₃₂ in.

PLATE 74

DESIGNS FOR SUMMER HOUSES AND SEA-SIDE COTTAGES.

Fig. 1.

Fig. 2.

Fig. 3

Fig. 4

Fig. 5.

Fig. 6.

Scale 3/32 in. = 1 foot

PLATE 75

FREE
COLORING PAGES, CLIP ART, PUZZLES & MORE!

Sign up for the Dover Sampler and you'll get an exclusive collection of fun activities delivered to your inbox each week. You can't get these free samples anywhere else!

The Sampler is completely free and it only takes a few seconds to sign up:

www.doverpublications.com/signupsampler

Are you a teacher? Sign up for FREE activities for your classroom! www.doverpublications.com/signupteachers

VICTORIAN ARCHITECTURAL DETAILS

Designs for Over 700 Stairs, Mantels, Doors, Windows, Cornices, Porches, and Other Decorative Elements

A. J. Bicknell & Company

Originally published well over a century ago by one of America's leading architectural firms, this volume provided prospective homeowners and other customers with a wide range of design alternatives. While the collection includes elevations and floor plans for a variety of handsome, private residences and commercial structures, the emphasis is on architectural details—from cornices to fireplace mantels.

Rare black-and-white illustrations depict designs for gable ornaments, fences, stairways, newel posts and hand rails, balconies, windows, front doors, porches, and chimney tops. Also included among the hundreds of illustrated details are designs for storefronts, banks, a barn, a Gothic cottage with tower, bridges, summer houses, and villas.

A valuable reference for home restorers, preservationists, and architectural historians, this book will delight anyone who appreciates the charm of Victorian architecture.

$11.95 USA   PRINTED IN THE USA

ISBN-13: 978-0-486-44015-6
ISBN-10: 0-486-44015-X

5 1 1 9 5

9 780486 440156

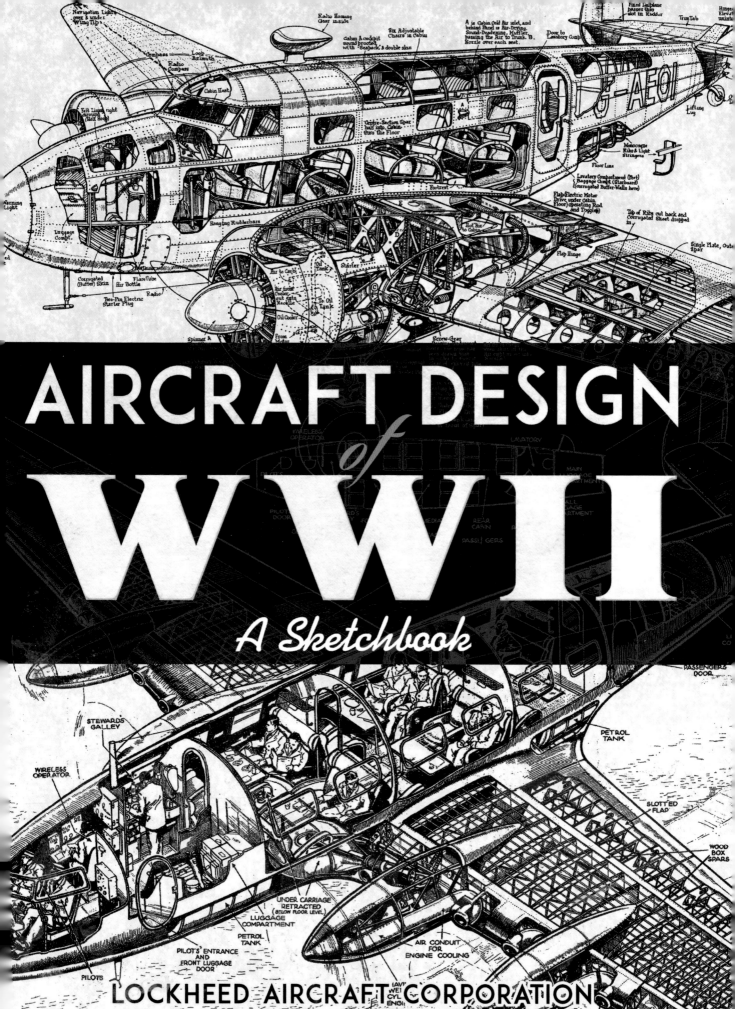

AIRCRAFT DESIGN

of

WWII

A Sketchbook

LOCKHEED AIRCRAFT CORPORATION

Dover Books on Military History

Civil War Hospital Sketches, Louisa May Alcott. (0-486-44900-9)

Civil War Stories, Ambrose Bierce. (0-486-28038-1)

Civil War Short Stories and Poems, Edited by Bob Blaisdell. (0-486-48226-X)

Civil War Letters: From Home, Camp and Battlefield, Edited by Bob Blaisdell. (0-486-48450-5)

World War One Short Stories, Edited by Bob Blaisdell. (0-486-48503-X)

The Gallic War, Julius Caesar. Translated by H. J. Edwards. (0-486-45107-0)

The Story of the Malakand Field Force, Winston Churchill. (0-486-47474-7)

Principles of War, Carl von Clausewitz. (0-486-42799-4)

Arms and Equipment of the Civil War, Jack Coggins. (0-486-43395-1)

Principles of Maritime Strategy, Julian S. Corbett. (0-486-43743-4)

The Fifteen Decisive Battles of the World: From Marathon to Waterloo, Sir Edward Shepherd Creasy. (0-486-46170-X)

Survival Handbook: The Official U.S. Army Guide, Department of the Army. (0-486-46184-X)

War Slang: American Fighting Words & Phrases Since the Civil War, Third Edition, Paul Dickson. With New Material on Iraq and Afghanistan by Ben Lando. (0-486-47750-9)

Civil War Adventure, Chuck Dixon and Gary Kwapisz. (0-486-79509-8)

Frederick Douglass on Slavery and the Civil War: Selections from His Writings, Frederick Douglass. (0-486-43171-1)

Posters of World Wars I and II CD-ROM and Book, Dover. (0-486-99684-0)

Sir Nigel: A Novel of the Hundred Years' War, Sir Arthur Conan Doyle. (0-486-47144-6)

An Encyclopedia of Battles: Accounts of Over 1,560 Battles from 1479 B.C. to the Present, David Eggenberger. (0-486-24913-1)

Photographic Sketch Book of the Civil War, Alexander Gardner. (0-486-22731-6)

The Dictionary of Espionage: Spyspeak into English, Joseph C. Goulden. New Foreword by Peter Earnest. (0-486-48348-7)

Personal Memoirs of U. S. Grant, Ulysses Simpson Grant. (0-486-28587-1)

Eavesdropping on Hell: Historical Guide to Western Communications Intelligence and the Holocaust, 1939-1945, Robert J. Hanyok. (0-486-48127-1)

Old Sword Play: Techniques of the Great Masters, Alfred Hutton. (0-486-41951-7)

Civil War Collector's Encyclopedia: Arms, Uniforms and Equipment of the Union and Confederacy, Francis A. Lord. (0-486-43660-8)

The Influence of Sea Power Upon History, 1660-1783, A. T. Mahan. (0-486-25509-3)

We Were There at the Battle of Gettysburg, Alida Sims Malkus. Illustrated by Leonard Vosburgh. (0-486-49261-3)

(continued on back flap)